HAUNTED
WHITBY

HAUNTED
WHITBY

ALAN BROOKE

The
History
Press

First published 2009

Reprinted 2012

The History Press
The Mill, Brimscombe Port
Stroud, Gloucestershire, GL5 2QG
www.thehistorypress.co.uk

British Library Cataloguing in Publication Data.
A catalogue record for this book is available from the British Library.

ISBN 978 0 7524 4925 8

Printed in Great Britain

CONTENTS

INTRODUCTION

Britain is reputed to be the most haunted country in the world. With its many castles, abbeys, graveyards, isolated moors, historic sites, pubs and large houses it has a rich seam of places to draw on. We might even add to that list tourist spots where the proliferation of ghost walks has made supernatural stories popular.

The Revd George Young (1777-1848), who lived in Whitby for over forty years and wrote *History of Whitby and Streoneshalh Abbey* (1817), commented that, 'Nowhere has superstition spread wider, or taken deeper root than in the neighbourhood of wealthy monasteries'. Whitby has a particularly unique atmosphere and it is no coincidence that Bram Stoker chose it as the location for Dracula's arrival in England. It was largely for this reason that Whitby became the choice for the Goth weekend festival which started in 1994 and has now become a twice yearly event held in April and October. The 'weekend' has grown to be one of the most popular Goth events in the world.

Despite the small population of Whitby and its relative seclusion, the town has a rich and fascinating history. It has many buildings, streets and places where tales of supernatural occurrences have been reported over the years. The majestic site of Whitby Abbey, which asserts a presence over the town, is the setting for a number of famous hauntings. The town also boasts one of the oldest ghost walks in the country.

Many ghost stories tend to be anecdotal and have been passed on from one generation to another. It is important that these stories are recorded and retold. There are many people who have not had a personal supernatural experience but the chances are that they know someone who has. Ghost stories fascinate and sometimes frighten us, but we decide what to accept or reject.

This is a book about hauntings and therefore it attempts to look at a broad range of supernatural phenomena, including ghosts. We tend to use a number of terms when describing a ghost – phantom, apparition or spirit. There is a brief section on page 14-15 which will define some of these terms. Not all aspects of the supernatural mentioned in this book are ghosts. There are many other sinister forces capable of haunting the living. Although some brief distinctions are made in this outline, the reader can find more comprehensive definitions in the many excellent encyclopedias on ghosts, spirits and the supernatural, such as *Chambers Dictionary of the Unexplained* (2007) or *The Encyclopaedia of Ghosts and Spirits* by Rosemary Guiley (2000).

This book is not concerned with proving or disproving the reality of ghosts. It is up to the reader to draw his or her own conclusions. Anyone wishing to pursue a serious historical study of ghosts should refer to the excellent book by Owen Davies, *Haunted: A Social History of Ghosts* (2007). As he states, 'whether you believe in ghosts or not, there is no doubt they make ideal guides for exploring the thoughts and emotions of our ancestors'. The subject of ghosts is always fascinating and offers us a mixture of suspense, fear, unaccountable happenings, mystery, unusual characters and creatures.

The accounts and stories in this book take various forms. There are those that are rooted in tradition in as much as different people have experienced them over many years. Others are based on the fleeting appearance of unexplained phenomena where individuals are strongly convinced of what they saw or heard. Some accounts in the book, such as the Dracula legend, are based on fiction but qualify for inclusion because they tell us something about Whitby as a wonderful setting for these ghoulish tales.

Importantly, the ghosts and ghouls recorded here are set within the context of a particular place and its history. Therefore a brief but informed historical background is essential to an understanding of a particular location such as the abbey, a house or a pub.

Further in the book there is an itinerary (which includes many additional tales) and a map of the town for anyone wishing to walk and locate the places that have been mentioned. There is also an A-Z of haunted places near to Whitby. Whitby is, and has always been, an isolated town but it is in close proximity to some of the most beautiful moorland, countryside, coastal villages and bays in the country.

This book owes a debt to the many people that have helped in making it possible. These include staff in the various archives of information – museums, libraries, newspapers and those who contributed stories and informed me of lesser-known aspects of Whitby and the surrounding area. Thanks go to family and friends for their continued support. A special thanks goes to Rod Corston (www.northernlightonline.com), a good friend of many years who kindly provided the photographs for this book.

One

WHITBY

Whitby is steeped in history and atmosphere. Whilst the town dates back to Roman times, its history mainly begins with the founding of the original abbey.

The town is situated on the north-east coast of Yorkshire and is divided by the River Esk. It neighbours the North York Moors National Park, which covers more than 500 miles², making it the largest area of heathland in England. A short distance to the north and the south are the fishing villages of Robin Hood's Bay, Staithes and Runswick. Many people will know Whitby as a fishing port and seaside resort with its piers, harbour, boats, sands, narrow streets and the ruins of its splendid abbey. Any visitor will be quickly aware of the town's nautical heritage, where there are reminders of this association everywhere.

On the east cliff overlooking the town is the wonderful haunting site of Whitby Abbey. Established as a royal monastery called Streaneshalch in the mid-seventh century, it was destroyed by Viking raiders but refounded after the Norman Conquest only to be dissolved in the sixteenth century after which it gradually fell into the ruins that we now see. The ruins provided the inspiration for one of the greatest horror novels ever written – Bram Stoker's *Dracula*. In fact, Whitby's place in literature was established from a much earlier period when the ploughboy Caedmon was acclaimed as the first poet in the English language. He died in Whitby in AD 680.

Whitby experienced a steady population growth over the centuries apart from moments of setback, such as the Black Death of 1349, which took its toll as it had done throughout the country. Thomas Langdale's *Yorkshire Dictionary* (1822) tells us that in 1540, during the reign of Henry VIII, Whitby consisted of only twenty to thirty houses with a population of around 200 inhabitants. Its population has fluctuated since then, rising from 3,000 in 1650 to a peak of over 14,000 in 1881, since when it has declined and now stands at around 12,000.

From the seventeenth and particularly the eighteenth century, the town prospered as a result of shipbuilding (by 1706, Whitby was the sixth-largest ship-building port in the UK), rope-making, sail-making, whaling and the coal trade between the Tyne and the Thames. When the first whaling ship set sail from Whitby in 1753 it marked the beginning of the growth of the town as a major centre for the whaling industry. This industry is commemorated by a large whalebone arch that stands at the top of the steps leading to West Cliff. Whitby has strong ties with Captain James Cook (1728-1779). It was here that the young James learnt his craft. He lodged as an apprentice and trained as a seaman, thus beginning the life of a sailor in 1747 on a ship carrying a cargo of coal to London. These early experiences would equip the great sailor and surveyor for his later epic voyages of discovery. Two of the ships he sailed on during his long voyages, *Resolution* and *Endeavour*, were built in Whitby.

In addition to the ship-building and fishing industry, a prosperous trade in alum production grew until its decline in the nineteenth century. There is an interesting story involving a curse connected with the advent of this industry. Sir Thomas Chaloner (1559-1615), textile entrepreneur, was responsible for introducing the mineral into Britain. Alum, a compound salt used in fixing dyed textiles and various other industrial processes, was important to Britain's textile industry. After a visit to Rome, Chaloner returned with some key Italian workers, who knew all the processes of alum manufacture. By 1600 his Belman works near Guisborough was in competition with the Pope's alum works in Rome. This brought great

Whitby Mission and Seafarers' Trust, Haggersgate House. One of many reminders of the town's association with fishing and the sea.

Haggersgate House

This early Georgian town house was built for the Walker Yeoman family. For several generations they were master mariners and ship-owners, involved in whaling and merchant shipping in many parts of the known world when Whitby was the seventh most important ship-owning town in England. The house was bought from their descendants in 1892 for use as a Mission to Seamen. In 1989 its charitable status was changed, and it became the Whitby Mission and Seafarers` Trust, for wider community use within the Parish of Whitby.

The plaque outside Haggersgate House.

The Captain Cook Statue on the West Cliff, which was unveiled in 1912.

Halfway up the 199 Steps, looking down.

anger from the Pope who called upon all holy institutions from 'God Almighty, the Father, Son and Holy Ghost' to rain curses on all those who spirited such expertise away from Italy.

However, it was largely the result of the building of the railway from the 1830s that attracted people to Whitby on a larger scale and with this came hotels and boarding houses, many of which were built on the West Cliff. Many middle-class visitors came, including the literary, artistic and professional classes who took advantage of the beach, rock pools or simply promenaded up and down or listened to the many bands. Not surprisingly, people such as Bram Stoker, Charles Dickens, Lewis Carroll, George Elliot, Alfred Lord Tennyson, Elizabeth Gaskell and others were attracted to Whitby.

During the mid-nineteenth century, Queen Victoria made Whitby jet jewellery fashionable and stimulated the expansion of the industry. Jet has its own mysteries and many years ago jet workers attributed unusual properties to the stone. The thin smoke that was produced from rubbing jet was believed to be an effective potent against spells, driving away the Devil and demons and curing people that had fallen victim to the 'evil eye'.

A famous landmark in Whitby is the 199 steps which date back to 1370 and connect the 900-year-old parish church of St Mary on the cliff top with the town and its narrow alleyways. The steps form the basis of a ghost story by Michel Faber, *The Hundred and Ninety-Nine Steps* (Canongate, 2002), which is based around an archaeological dig at the abbey. Despite Dracula being a fictional character, many visitors still climb the steps to look for his grave in St Mary's churchyard. In the book, Mina Murray, a young schoolmistress and central character, records in her journal that the parish church has a 'big graveyard full of tombstones' and adds that it is the 'nicest spot in Whitby' because of its view over the harbour and the town. Anyone visiting the spot would agree with her observations, but it is certainly not the resting place of Dracula, who would have hated the idea of a Christian burial.

The association with the sea has played a large part in Whitby's history and it has also been the basis of many myths and legends. Nautical superstitions abound in the traditions of the fishing communities far beyond the town. An article in the *Whitby Repository* in 1828 commented upon the abundance of local tales, maritime or otherwise, when it noted that:

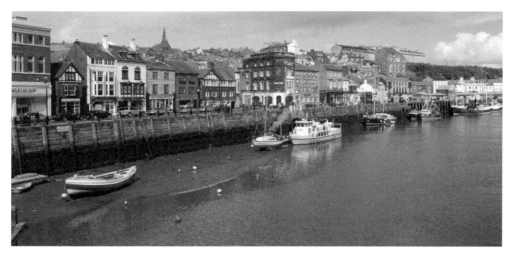

Boats in the harbour reflect Whitby's long fishing heritage.

> Whitby people are extremely addicted to superstitious practices – dreams, and various other every-day occurrences, are regarded by them as indicatory of future events; certain days are looked upon as fortunate or unfortunate, and almost every commonplace incident in life is considered as having its ominous tendency, good or evil.

It also added that all classes and ages hold such beliefs. In the scary tale, *Oh, Whistle, and I'll Come to You My Lad* (1904), M.R. James (1862-1936), the great writer of English ghost stories, supported this view when one of the characters in the story said: 'They believe in … [superstition] all over Denmark and Norway, as well as on the Yorkshire coast; and my experience is, mind you, that there's generally something at the bottom of what these country-folk hold to, and have held to for generations.'

Many of the superstitions outlined in the *Whitby Repository* could be found among Whitby folk, especially fishermen and sailors. Names, appearances, days and seasons could determine when to sail and when not to sail. It was believed that Friday was the worst possible day to start a journey on a boat and no enterprise could succeed which commenced on that day. Work that began on a Saturday would require seven more Saturdays before completion, while a job started on Monday was always likely to be finished quickly. Sunday was a lucky day, yet there was a firm conviction among many that it was unlucky to fish on a Sunday. Certain animals and people were so unlucky it was believed that they must never be named, such as a pig or a rat. It was considered unlucky to shoot nets on the port side, or to taste food before any fish had been caught. An encyclopaedia of superstitions in 1949 stated that no old Yorkshire fisherman, especially if he came from Whitby, would think of going out in his boat if his boots had been carried on the shoulder of a boy. It also added that Yorkshire sailors and fishermen who claimed to see a woman in a white apron as they went down the quay in the morning would, without fail, turn around. Victorian writers mention children around Whitby lighting fires on the cliff top during a storm and dancing and singing:

> Souther Wind, souther,
> And Blow father home to mother.

The coastal areas around Whitby, such as Staithes, Ravenscar and Robin Hood's Bay, have had a long tradition with smuggling. Reports of such activity were not uncommon. For example, on 31 December 1785 *The Times* reported that, 'We hear from Whitby, that several smuggling vessels have lately been upon the coast in that neighbourhood, and have landed great quantities of spirits …' On 31 August 1790 the paper wrote that a 'smuggling lugger, with a thousand ankers and half ankers of rum, brandy, and geneva,

A narrow winding street in Robin Hood's Bay.

to the amount of 6000 gallons, was taken and sent into Whitby ...' Skinner Street was considered to be the hub of this clandestine trade.

Local smugglers in the late eighteenth century would wait off the coast until the fishermen sailed out in their small boats to pick up the contraband goods. In Robin Hood's Bay, 6 miles south of Whitby, houses and inns had connecting cellars where goods used to be smuggled out. In 1856 coastguard men were given the job of stopping the smuggling at Robin Hood's Bay and Whitby, but they faced so much opposition that the Dragoons were brought in to help. A well-known meeting place for smugglers was Cockmill where they would indulge in drinking and gambling. One tale emanating from these gatherings told of how the Devil – or the Gentleman in Black as he was referred to – sat among the smugglers and played a hand of cards. How did the smugglers know it was the Devil? If any of them happened to drop their cards on the floor, on bending down to pick them up they would see two cloven feet under the table.

Smuggling has its own associations with ghosts, although these links were often created as diversionary tactics from the excise men. Robin Hood's Bay provides some interesting examples of such stories. The Bay, with its narrow streets, cliff-clinging cottages and history of fishing and smuggling, is a popular haunt of visitors and walkers. One story concerns that of the ghost of Lingers Hill. The 'ghost', a figure (known to be a local farmer) in a white sheet riding on a horse between Robin Hood's Bay and neighbouring Fylingthorpe, was used to frighten people away from the streets on the nights when a smuggling run was about to take place.

Today, fishing around the area is conducted on a fairly small scale. Tourism is a key industry and Whitby makes proud use of its heritage with the cobblestone streets and winding passages of the Old Town, the abbey and museum, the ghost walks and the Dracula association.

WHAT ARE GHOSTS?

G hosts have haunted the imagination of the English for centuries. They have been popular in literature, film, stories, plays and currently in the many television programmes dedicated to the supernatural. People have been fascinated and frightened by the idea of an afterlife and the possibility of the souls of the dead still walking among the living. Despite the advance of science and scepticism since the eighteenth century there continues to be an interest in ghosts. According to a poll conducted by ICM in 2004, 42 per cent of the population said they believed in ghosts. What is remarkable is that this figure is 30 per cent higher than polls that were carried out by Gallup in the 1950s.

The dictionary usually defines a ghost as the soul of a dead person, a disembodied spirit wandering among or haunting living persons or former habitats. Ghosts have become lost or stuck between this plane of existence and the next, and because they are lost they are not aware that they are dead. Sceptics argue that experiences of ghosts are simply the products of our own minds. We see ghosts because we want to see them, as in the case of some people suffering bereavement. Whitby historian George Young wrote in very sceptical terms, stating that, 'it would be an endless task to detail all the absurd local traditions and all the haunted houses in the district'. Percy Shaw Jeffrey (*Whitby Lore and the Legend*) also drew attention to such beliefs when he quoted an article in the *Whitby Repository* (1828), noting that:

> Apparitions both before and after death, are of course not unfrequent (sic) in Whitby. Many a valuable house has stood untenanted for years on the suspicion of its being haunted … Strange traditions exist of certain yards, lanes, and alleys; of some terrible homicide there committed; of departed spirits that have walked for several nights successively, deprived of their rest, desirous of being addressed by someone, but none daring; of hearses and mourning coaches that have been seen to drive past at midnight, the horses without heads or both with white sheets on their backs; and numerous other equally credible reports; the whole of which most of the inhabitants fearfully believe.

The word ghost has a variety of associations: apparition, phantom, wraith, revenant, poltergeist, spook, spectre and spirit. Despite the similarity there are degrees of difference. An 'apparition' is the supernatural appearance of a person or thing – a ghost-like presence which may appear only once. It might also be a religious vision. A 'crisis apparition' is when a vision appears before a person, usually someone close such as a friend or relative. The vision is seen at a moment when they are undergoing some form of crisis such as a serious illness, an injury or even death. The recipient learns at a later stage that the person actually died. These cases are quite eerie and have some conviction largely because the person who saw the vision tells someone else before the death is confirmed.

The term 'wraith', first used in 1513, has evolved and taken on a number of meanings. The type of wraith discussed in this book refers to the reflected image (a double) of a person seen immediately before their death. There are a number of stories relating to wraiths in Whitby.

A 'revenant' is the spirit of a person who returns after a lengthy absence. Revenants also reflect the belief that if the dead are not buried properly, they will not be able to find their way into the other-world or might even be barred from entering it.

A 'poltergeist' is a ghost or spirit which manifests its presence by noises and knockings. Poltergeists are also blamed for hiding objects, throwing things across rooms or even pulling people's clothing or hair and scratching the living. Such malicious spirits have haunted a number of places around Whitby including Runswick Bay and Upleatham. These small, grotesque supernatural spirits, which have also been referred to as hobgoblins, usually make trouble for human beings. In medieval times they were associated with the Devil. We might also include fairies in this category because in the past they were not the diminutive, benign beings that children today tend to think of.

Many people have experienced what might be described as ghost lights – mysterious lights usually in the form of white or blue balls or yellow spheres. Most of these sightings have been attributed to swamp gas, electricity or some phosphorescent material. There has been, in recent years, a proliferation of these lights or 'orbs' because of digital photographs.

Three

THE NATURE OF GHOSTS AND HAUNTED PLACES

G hosts and hauntings take many forms. A particular place – a house, church or road – can be haunted not only by a ghost but also by other supernatural phenomena. The nearest anyone has come to capturing a ghost is on film and the authenticity of such images has often been disputed. It is unusual for more than one person to see a ghost at the same time.

Why should ghosts want to haunt the living? For some, the souls of the dead cannot rest because of some terrible way in which they ended their lives, such as murder or suicide. Other restless spirits might come back to haunt those who had not been true to the last wishes of the deceased or because there was some other score to settle. The Revd J.C. Atkinson (1814-1900), vicar of Danby, whose books include *Memorials of Old Whitby* and *Forty Years in a Moorland Parish*, noted that ghosts were likely to return if the corpse was not conveyed along the old traditional road to the burial ground.

In the medieval period ghost stories were regularly told and it was important that the Church conveyed certain messages about the sacraments, the forgiveness for sins and the ways in which the living might assist the dead through prayers, masses and alms-giving. The Catholic Church taught that ghosts were the souls of those trapped in purgatory (a halfway stage after death between earth and Heaven), unable to rest until they had suffered for their sins. It was believed that a ghost would avenge the living that betrayed their last dying wish. The inscription on the grave of William Shakespeare (1564-1616) in the Church of Holy Trinity, Stratford-Upon-Avon, offers such a warning:

> Good friend, for Jesus' sake forebeare
> To digg the dust enclosed heare;
> Bleste be the man that spares these stones,
> And curst be he that moves my bones

Most people in medieval England believed in ghosts and accepted that the dead might return to haunt the living. The Church often manipulated and perpetuated such beliefs. With the Reformation of the sixteenth century, which saw the decline of Catholicism and the rise of Protestantism, the belief in purgatory was attacked as superstitious nonsense. However, this did not end the belief in the afterlife or ghosts, and many old and new sightings of apparitions flourished.

Before the nineteenth century it was usual for people to want to banish ghosts by various means, such as exorcisms. However, from the nineteenth century a change in attitude towards ghosts occurred. With the rise of spiritualism and the growth of mediums it became more fashionable to want to contact the dead. Rather than make a spirit materialise, mediums attempted to transmit messages from the dead to the family or friends. The Fraudulent Mediums Act of 1951, which repealed the Witchcraft Act of 1735, was introduced to punish persons who 'fraudulently purport to act as spiritualistic mediums or to exercise powers of telepathy, clairvoyance or other similar powers'.

Are ghosts seen all year round or more often at certain times of the year? In medieval England they were often seen in the period between Christmas and Epiphany (the Twelfth Day – 6 January), although

A view down Haggersgate where the phantom coach could be heard.

this may be due to the midwinter darkness. Even down to our own times ghosts are associated with the night or dark places such as cellars or tunnels.

Ghosts will continue to haunt a building even when that structure has been demolished and replaced by another. They are not only detectable by their visual presence but in some cases they have noticeable smells. There is a case in Scarborough, where a ghost leaves behind a strong smell of perfume in a room. For the most part, throughout history ghosts are not usually dressed in black although the shadow of them might give that impression. It is believed that when a soul passed through purgatory it changed from black to white.

Sightings of headless ghosts, animals and noisy poltergeist also feature among supernatural phenomena, and Whitby can claim to have all of these in its ghost lore. Noisy hauntings were documented as long ago as the twelfth century. William of Newburgh (1136-1198), an English historian, Yorkshireman and Augustinian canon, recounted in his famous *Historia rerum Anglicarum* (History of English Affairs) the stories he had heard from around north-east Yorkshire about revenants. William considered such accounts to be a contemporary plague, adding that there were so many tales that it would be tedious to record all the instances he had heard. Revenants were wrongdoers – wicked, vain or unbelievers – who returned from the dead. They were associated with spreading disease and the only way to be rid of them was exhumation followed by decapitation, burning or removal of the heart. Interestingly, some accounts have implied that they sucked blood and were described as vampires, which adds a particular dimension to Whitby's association with Dracula.

Religious buildings have provided a rich source of ghostly goings on. Another Yorkshire account of noisy ghosts comes from a Cistercian monk at Byland Abbey around 1400, who told of the dead appearing in order to make amends for the sins they had committed in life, such as murder or theft. Such spirits, according to the monk, desired the living to free their souls from purgatory by paying for their sins to be absolved. These ghosts were capable of shape shifting into animal form.

Whitby has a number of ghost animals, although there is a debate over whether animals have souls. A particularly common sighting in a number of areas, including Whitby, is of a large black dog, which according to some accounts is the Devil in disguise. Not surprising then that the appearance of such a creature brings with it a diabolic and terrifying encounter and a forewarning of death.

How long do ghosts exist? Do most spirits appear before family or friends for a short time and then go away for all eternity? A general view is that spirits make a one-off appearance shortly after their death to people close to them in order to bring messages of comfort. Do ghosts only haunt one particular place? The Dick Turpin ghost reputedly frequents many pubs between York and London! The persistence of tales over many years may be more to do with the transmission of collective storytelling through time. Nonetheless, some sightings persist, such as the ghost of St Hilda of Whitby Abbey who died in AD 680 and has been reputedly seen or heard down to recent times.

Finally, can inanimate objects, such as bells, hearses, coaches, ships and clothing (all common to Whitby ghost stories), take on a ghost-like appearance? After all, such objects do not possess consciousness and were never 'alive'. Why should a ghost choose to wear particular types of clothing? Although many people were buried in shrouds they are often seen wearing everyday clothing. It is rare to see a ghost in the all-together. The afterlife would be a very cluttered place if items of clothing as well as untold types of objects resided there. One explanation suggests that inanimate objects are mirages or pre-recorded impressions of some kind, rather than actual manifestations. Another holds that ghosts have the ability to represent to the viewer whatever they want to see, and clothes are an important item of identity, especially when it comes to recognizing a ghost from a particular period in the past. Some inanimate objects are only heard rather than seen, such as the phantom coach of Haggersgate in Whitby.

During the late twentieth century, stories of old ghosts were revived on a huge scale as a result of the media, the proliferation of paranormal groups and the growth of tourism. It seems that it is still as much a part of our culture as it was in the medieval period.

Four

WHITBY ABBEY AND ITS GHOSTS

The ruins of Whitby Abbey provide an ideal setting for ghost stories. Instantly recognisable in photographs and paintings, the abbey perches on the cliff top, standing as an iconic symbol of Whitby. For centuries the ruins have formed a conspicuous landmark both inland and far out to sea. Its majestic presence also symbolises the power of the early church. The starting point for most histories of Whitby begin with the abbey. Founded as a monastery in AD 657 with a mixed community of men and women, it flourished under the rule of Abbess Hilda (Hild was the Anglo-Saxon name during her lifetime), and attracted future bishops and the first-known English religious poet, Caedmon. Whitby Abbey, originally called Streaneshalch Abbey, became one of the foremost religious centres in England. Although destroyed by the Vikings in 867, the Normans rebuilt it 200 years later, in 1067.

The famous Synod (meeting) of AD 664 was held there. This involved the coming together of the two branches of early English Christianity, the Celtic and Roman Churches, to debate Church policy, including the important issue of the dating of Easter. The crucial issue was which religious tradition England would follow – the Church of Rome or the Celtic Church of Ireland. The Synod decided in favour of the Roman tradition, which ruled until the Reformation of the sixteenth century. After the dissolution of the abbey in 1539, the destruction began. In 1580 it passed to the Cholmley family who built a mansion largely out of materials plundered from the monastery. Parts of this building have been incorporated into the nineteenth-century Abbey House. The abbey suffered further damage in 1830 when the central tower collapsed, and again on 16 December 1914 when two German cruisers demolished part of the Western Arch. Unfortunately, Whitby, along with Hartlepool and Scarborough, was one of the few British towns to suffer bombardment during the First World War. When the Crown took control of the ruins in 1920, there had been considerable damage. Needless to say the area around the abbey is not without its dead. Archaeological excavations in 1925 found remains of an Anglo-Saxon cemetery and in 1958 several skeletons were revealed, presumed to be part of the lay cemetery of the thirteenth century. In 1999-2000 another excavation exposed part of a massive Anglo-Saxon cemetery.

St Hilda

It is with St Hilda that tales of ghostly sightings are first recorded at Whitby Abbey. Saint Hilda (614-680), a royal princess, was a great niece of Edwin, King of Northumbria, and the second daughter of Hereric, Edwin's nephew. Interestingly, the headless body of King Edwin (586-633) was a notable burial at Whitby. He had been killed at the Battle of Hatfield (633) and his body was found later covered with blood, dirt and gore. His head, which had been removed, was later brought to the newly built Chapel of St Gregory in York Minster, whilst his body was sent to the monastery at Whitby.

Hilda died at the age of sixty-six after spending over twenty years at the abbey. Years earlier she converted to Christianity and served in an East Anglian monastery. In 649 she was appointed Abbess of Hartlepool before coming to the newly established monastery in Whitby in 657, where she would spend the rest of her life. When Hilda arrived in Whitby at the age of forty-three, she was said to have carried out

The ruins of Whitby Abbey.

her appointment with great energy and built up a thriving and well-established community. Testimony to this is the decision to hold the Synod there. She was an excellent teacher as well as abbess and ruler of her monastery. The great eighth-century English historian Bede (673-735) wrote in his *Ecclesiastical History of the English People* (731) that she 'taught there the strict observance of justice, piety, chastity, and other virtues, and particularly of peace and charity'. Bede adds that her prudence was so great, that both 'indifferent persons' and kings and princes 'asked and received her advice'. Hilda set an example of good life not only 'to those that lived in her monastery', but also to those who 'lived at a distance'. At the age of sixty she succumbed to a fever from which she was afflicted on and off for the next six years, and she died – or as Bede put it, she passed 'from death to life.'

Bede told of two visions related to Hilda's death. On the same night as her death a strange apparition appeared in another monastery at Hackness some 13 miles away. A nun by the name of Begu, who had devoted some thirty years of her life in the monastery, was woken from her sleep by the sound of a bell. As she opened her eyes she saw the roof open, and a strong light poured in from above. Clearly alarmed, she saw a ghost-like figure. It was the soul of St Hilda floating as if ascending into Heaven. Begu, who was sleeping in the remotest part of the monastery, clambered from her bed with great fright and ran to tell of her vision to one of the other nuns. With many tears and sighs, the nun told her that the Abbess Hilda had departed this life, and had ascended to eternal bliss. Begu had reputedly seen the soul of Hilda ascend to Heaven in the company of angels and this vision, she declared, took place at the very same hour that Hilda had passed away. It was as though Begu had experienced a crisis apparition – the image of someone about to die; or in this case, someone who had just died.

It is said that St Hilda never left the abbey, despite a twelfth-century chronicle which tells of Hilda's bones being removed by King Edmund in 944 and taken to Glastonbury. Whether this is true or not her ghost certainly stayed in the abbey grounds and has been sighted on many occasions. The ghost of Hilda wrapped in a shroud is believed to appear frequently in one of the abbey's highest windows. An extract from a poem quoted in the book, *The Old Seaport of Whitby* (1909) by Robert Tate Gaskin, suggests the precise location of Hilda's ghost:

... the abbey now you see
I made that you might think of me

Ammonite fossils – or, according to legend, the petrified remains of snakes which Hilda decapitated with her whip and banished over the cliff edge.

Also a window there I plac'd
That you might see me as undress'd
In morning gown a nightrail, there
All the day long fairly appear;
At the west end of church you'll see,
Nine paces there in each degree ...

Presumably Hilda's ghost must have moved from the site of the original monastery where she had lived to the abbey. It is thought that the monastery, which was probably made from wattle and daub, was situated on or near the present site of St Mary's Church which stands close to the present abbey.

There is also a legend that associates Hilda with ammonite fossils and snakes. Whitby's coastline is referred to as the 'dinosaur coast' because of the many fossils that can be found there. According to the legend the ammonites are the petrified remains of snakes that once plagued the Whitby area until Hilda turned them into stone. She drove them to the cliff's edge and decapitated them with her whip. The English historian William Camden (1551-1623) made reference to snakestones in his book *Britannia* (1586). He states that the coastline around Robin Hood's Bay to Whitby are found 'certain stones fashioned like serpents folded and wrapped round as in a wreathe ... A man would think they had been sometime serpents, which a coat or crust of stone had now covered all over.'

There is another mystery in relation to Hilda's legendary powers and one that Camden also mentions. He wrote that people spoke of how wild geese flying over the area would suddenly fall down to the ground. He acknowledged that he would not have believed such a story had it not come from persons who were 'not given to superstitious credulity'. Why did the geese fall from the sky? According to Camden, the reason was attributed to a 'secret propriety of this ground, and to a hidden dissent between this soil and those geese'. The lack of seagulls flying over the abbey ruins, according to legend, is because Hilda forbade them and those that strayed over the abbey grounds are said to dip their wings in respect. An extract from the poem *Marmion* (1808) by Sir Walter Scott (1771-1832) acknowledged this:

They told of how sea-fowls' pinions fail,
As over Whitby's towers they sail,
And, sinking down, with flutterings faint,
They do their homage to their saint.
(Canto 2, verse XIII)

St Cuthbert

Another alleged reason for the headless snakestones at Whitby is because of a beheading curse cast by St Cuthbert of Lindisfarne (635-687). St Cuthbert's beads are carboniferous crinoids strung together like a necklace. The legend states that Cuthbert either used the beads as a rosary or that his spirit created them on stormy nights so they could be found on the beach the next day. The origin of this legend is unclear and references go back to the seventeenth century. There is also a passage in *Marmion* which states:

But fain Saint Hilda's nuns would learn
If, on a rock by Linisfarne,
Saint Cuthbert sits, and toils beads that bear his name:
Such tales Whitby's fishers told
And said might his shape behold,
And here his anvil sound:
A deadened clang – a huge dim form
Seen but and heart when gathering storm
(Canto 2, verse XVI)

A few years after the death of St Hilda, the aged St Cuthbert, now 'foreseeing his end', had decided to visit the houses of the faithful in his neighbourhood. When he came to Whitby he met Hilda's successor, Abbess Elfleda. As they were dining Cuthbert was suddenly struck by a ghostly apparition. At first he tried to conceal the fact that he had seen something supernatural, and replied, 'I was not able to eat the whole day.' The abbess, not satisfied with his answer, persisted to ask what terrified him. He then replied, 'I saw the soul of a man.' The abbess asked, 'From what place was it taken?' Cuthbert responded, 'From your monastery.' Elfreda immediately inquired at the monastery if anyone had died. Although no one was accounted for, it was not long after that a messenger suddenly met some men carrying a body that was just about to be buried in a cart. On enquiring who it was, the messenger was told that it was one of the shepherds, a man named Hadwald, who had died falling from a tree. This was the man Cuthbert claimed he had seen.

Caedmon's Vision

Many abbeys employed local farm servants who worked on the monastic lands, and one such elderly servant at Whitby was the poet Caedmon, one of Whitby's great sons. Caedmon was a modest, even shy man whose life was concerned with tending to cattle and livestock. Bede writes of Caedmon as a man who interpreted 'Scripture into poetical expressions of much sweetness and humility, in English, which was his native language.' Unfortunately, none of his poems have survived save for nine lines in Latin recorded by Bede. Caedmon acquired his gift as a result of a vision. He was never one given to socialising and singing songs, and when it came to a drinking session Caedmon, conscious of his inability to sing, would depart.

It was his departure from one particular social occasion that changed his life dramatically. At this event he left the banquet hall and went out to the animal stables when he felt the need to rest his limbs and he soon fell asleep. During his slumber a man appeared asking Caedmon to sing. The man said 'Caedmon, sing some song to me.' He answered, 'I cannot sing; for that was the reason why I left the entertainment, and retired to this place'. The vision replied, 'You shall sing.' 'What shall I sing?' Caedmon asked. 'Sing the beginning of created beings,' said the other. Caedmon then began to compose verses in Old English that

Caedmon Cross in Celtic design, erected in 1898 to commemorate the first English poet. It includes the figures of Christ, David, Abbess Hilda and Caedmon.

he had never heard, and the next morning he told the reeve – a steward responsible for parish affairs – of his new gift. Caedmon was taken to the abbess and many learned men, to whom he told his story and sang for them. From that moment he was invited to join the monastic community, in which he stayed until his death in 680.

At the end of his life Caedmon knew his death was imminent, despite being engaged in the enjoyable company of others. He suddenly asked for the Blessed Eucharist, which surprised the brothers who asked why he needed this as he was in good health and not about to die. In fact, he was enjoying the merriment of their company. Nonetheless, Caedmon persisted in his request, saying that, 'I am in charity, my children, with all the servants of God'. That night he signed himself with the sign of the cross 'laid his head on the pillow, and falling into a slumber, ended his life in silence'.

Other Abbey Hauntings

The story of the ghost of Constance de Beverley, a young Whitby nun who is said to haunt the abbey ruins, would be a great tale if it were true. It is said that she was bricked up alive in a dungeon in Whitby Abbey, and her ghost has been seen on the winding stairway leading from the dungeon, cowering and begging release. It is even mentioned in *Dracula*:

> Over the town is the ruin of Whitby Abbey … which is the scene of part of 'Marmion,' where the girl was built up in the wall. It is a most noble ruin, of immense size, and full of beautiful and romantic bits. There is a legend that a white lady is seen in one of the windows.

The tale of Constance comes from the poem *Marmion*, a tale of *Flodden Field* (1808) by Sir Walter Scott, and tells of Lord Marmion, a favourite of Henry VIII, who lusts after a rich woman, Clara de Clare. Marmion and his mistress, Constance de Beverley, a dishonest nun, forge a letter implicating Clara's fiancé Sir Ralph De Wilton in treason:

> De Wilton and Lord Marmion woo'd
> Clara de Clare, of Gloster's blood;

By helping him Constance hopes that Marmion will favour her, but it was not to be, as Marmion abandons her and she is cast out and ends up dying an awful death:

> Still was false Marmion's bridal staid;
> To Whitby's convent fled the maid,
> The hated match to shun …
> With Clare alone he credence won,
> Who, rather than wed Marmion,
> Did to Saint Hilda's shrine repair,
> To give our house her livings fair,
> And die a vestal vot'ress there.
> The impulse from the earth was given,
> But bent her to the paths of heaven.
> A purer heart, a lovelier maid,
> Ne'er shelter'd her in Whitby's shade,

Later in the poem, we learn of the voyage of the Whitby nuns along the rockbound Durham and Northumbrian coasts to St Cuthbert's Holy Island and the trial which condemned Constance to the dreaded vault of Lindisfarne. Marmion hears from Clare that Constance died a bitter death at Lindisfarne:

> Forgive and listen, gentle Clare!
> 'Alas!' she said, 'the while,
> O, think of your immortal weal!
> In vain for Constance is your zeal;
> She-died at Holy Isle.'
> Lord Marmion started from the ground,
> … 'Then it was truth,' he said. 'I knew
> That the dark presage must be true.'

The poem also contains the very famous and well-known lines when Marmion says:

> I … Must separate Constance from the Nun
> O, what a tangled web we weave,
> When first we practise to deceive!

Other ghostly experiences in the abbey grounds include a more recent account of some treasure hunters who were in search of rich pickings from around the abbey – or maybe they were after the hidden fortune that, according to myth and legend, is buried within the grounds. As the hopeful searchers dug around in the ruins an eerie mist descended around them. The two men started to feel uncomfortable and were probably wishing they were somewhere safer. Suddenly they held their breath (and maybe other expressions resulting from terror) as they felt the tap of a hand on their shoulders. They turned around and to their horror saw a headless figure clad in white standing over them. The men had clearly disturbed the sanctity of the abbey and the ghostly figure was a terrifying warning to them to be more respectful. No doubt they quickly gave up their searches for the treasure.

Another strange occurrence often reported within the vicinity of the abbey is the sound of bells ringing or choirs singing when no one is present. This phenomenon is associated with a number of cathedrals, abbeys and churches in England, and Whitby is no exception. Over the years, people have claimed that whilst they have been in the area of the abbey they have heard the faint echoes of a choir gently drifting across the grounds very early on a Christmas morning, even though no one else is there.

Holy Island – was this the place where Constance de Beverley died?

The Abbey Bells

The sound of church bells is very evocative and for most people they normally signify a service, marriage, death, funeral or national celebration. In previous times they would also ring to signal curfews. However, there was always great superstition associated with bells. They were anointed with holy oil and blessed by the bishop. They also contained inscriptions in order to make them a more powerful talisman against evil. These rituals derived from a belief that when these ceremonies had been performed, bells had the power to drive away the Devil and all his hosts who feared the sound of a church bell. The bells of Whitby Abbey, it seems, proved very powerful in acting against those who tried to take them.

A well-known story concerns the old bells that were taken during the Reformation. These bells, which went down in a sunken ship bound for London, have been heard over the centuries still ringing out from the sea where they were lost.

Following the decision by Henry VIII's Parliament to break away from the Roman Catholic faith in the 1530s, the process of dissolving the great abbeys and monastic houses of their wealth began in order that Henry could enrich his coffers and get rid of any pockets of Catholic resistance. The annual value of Whitby Abbey was estimated at £437 2s 9d. In December 1539, Abbot Henry de Vall and eighteen monks surrendered the abbey to the King's commissioners. This then started the process of dismantling and destruction that saw the roof stripped of its lead. Other parts were used for the roof of St Mary's Church, which as the Whitby historian Percy Shaw Jeffrey stated, 'seemed only to have had a thatched roof.' Further despoiling took place as the bells of the abbey, which were described as 'very noble and antique', were sold and ordered to be sent to London by sea. The local inhabitants were clearly distraught at losing the historic bells to which they had become accustomed to hearing.

After the bells had been loaded onto the ship and were ready to face the voyage south, the ship set sail on what was a calm sea. As it left the harbour it had sailed no more than a mile when a most extraordinary event happened. The ship began to sink slowly, possibly as a result of the weight of its sacrilegious plunder. However, there were many people who believed the sinking was a consequence of unexplained powers that had intervened to make sure the bells did not leave Whitby. Whatever the reason, it seemed that fate had conspired to make sure that the bells did not reach their destination. Percy Shaw Jeffrey tells us that 'the sorrowing crowds that lined the cliffs' to the 'end of 'Black Nab' – approximately a mile from the abbey – looked on in astonishment as the ship, along with the bells, sunk to the bottom of the sea where they remained. However, this was not to be the end of the story. On quiet nights people have heard the bells ringing out from the sea that took them.

There are other tales associated with the sinking of the bells. One suggests that love-struck youngsters would climb the tower of St Mary's Church next to the abbey and shout the name of their loved one out to sea. Their wish would come true if the bells sounded. Let's hope that many did not wait too long in vain to hear the bells. Another tale tells of how the haunting peal of the bells was heard by a pirate who, with his crew, found the bells and carried them away on his ship – no mean feat given the weight of this treasure. However, the bells one again wreaked their revenge. The ship had not travelled far when it struck a rock and sank with all hands, as well as the bells.

It is said that if a Whitby ship is in danger, or a Whitby seaman dies at sea, the bells ring as if lamenting the loss. In Bram Stoker's *Dracula*, Mina Murray, the fiancé of Jonathan Harker and initially a victim of Count Dracula, makes reference to the story in her journal (chapter 6 of *Dracula*) when she visits Whitby: 'They have a legend here that when a ship is lost bells are heard out at sea. I must ask the old man about this.'

The loss of church or abbey bells is a recurrent theme in other places. Tales of curses, phantom ringing, falling into deep water, bells leading people to safety or as omens of death are told in many parts of England. It seems that bells have a habit of protesting when they are mistreated.

Five

THE BARGUEST

One of the most terrifying of supernatural creatures is the monstrous phantom dog, the black hound that stalks the moors or dark streets looking for unsuspecting victims. Such a creature – the Barguest (or Barguest) – looms large in Whitby's haunted history. The origin of the term is unclear but one suggestion is that the word 'ghost' in the north of England was once pronounced 'guest', and 'burgh' was 'town', hence 'burgh-gest' – town ghost. Another variation on this is bar – the first syllable – meaning bier, a stand for a coffin.

J.C. Atkinson wrote in *The Last of the Giant Killers* (1891) of a very gruesome kind of being which had a number of different names according to the very many places in which it was seen or heard:

> I have heard it called Pad-foot, because of the strange muffled sound of its feet when it met or passed people in the dusk of the evening, or later in the still of the night. Others used to call the beast 'Scriker,' because of the awful scrikes [shrieks] it uttered when out on its terrible errand of death, for someone was sure to die soon after it had been seen or heard.

Such spectral hounds are said to exist in other parts of Britain such as Lancashire, Cornwall, Devon, Norfolk, Suffolk, Essex and the north of England. The hound goes by various names: Black Shuck, Shug Monkey, Hellbeast, Gwyllgi, Black Dog, Padfoot, and Scriker. Sightings have been consistent over the centuries down to recent times. Anyone who catches sight of the Barguest is likely to die, as these creatures are omens of death and are said to strike down anyone (and their family) who witnesses them. There are differing accounts as to the origins of this hell hound. One view suggests they are related to the days of smuggling, when fears of a large spectral dog roaming the coastal areas at night were sufficient reason for people to stay indoors while smugglers conducted their activities. An early account of the beast features in the twelfth-century *Anglo-Saxon Chronicle*. Other accounts suggest that the stories are rooted in Norse mythology and entered Britain with the early Viking raiders.

Although Black Dogs appear in many paranormal experiences throughout Britain, the accounts and descriptions are very similar. The Barguest roams coastlines, graveyards, country roads, misty marshes and moors (as in *The Hound of the Baskervilles*). They are, according to accounts, a frightening sight to behold and are described as being the size of a calf, having a sulphurous smell, jet-black hair, large teeth and claws, and eyes that glow yellow and green, but mainly red as if on fire. So large and scary are the eyes, they have been described as 'big as saucers'. Known for their shape-shifting, the hound is also capable of vanishing altogether. Sometimes they can be seen near bridges or crossroads or on old trackways said to be ley lines – alignments between ancient monuments which are believed to resonate psychic energy – but the creature leaves no trace of their tracks. Given that the largest wild carnivore native to Britain is the fox, followed by badgers and wildcats, could it be that we face the prospect of a new carnivore in Britain, of unknown origin?

The most terrifying feature of the Barguest is their bone-chilling howl that can be heard above the wind, even on stormy nights. It is also said that the dogs are associated with the Devil, who can take on the shape of a black dog. In the classic book, Count Dracula leapt ashore at Whitby sands from the ship

The Barghest – the large, panther-like black dog and harbinger of doom which has haunted areas in and around Whitby. Described as jet black with red eyes, it was also the shape that Dracula took when he arrived from the ship in Whitby.

Demeter in the form of an immense dog. Bram Stoker drew on many of the features associated with the legend such as an eerie wind, a lonely graveyard, desolate moors, a hound disappearing into the dark and the ferocity of the beast:

> The wind suddenly shifted to the northeast, and the remnant of the sea fog melted in the blast … The searchlight followed her, and a shudder ran through all who saw her, for lashed to the helm was a corpse, with drooping head, which swung horribly to and fro at each motion of the ship. No other form could be seen on the deck at all.
>
> A great awe came on all as they realised that the ship, as if by a miracle, had found the harbour, unsteered save by the hand of a dead man! However, all took place more quickly than it takes to write these words. The schooner … pitched herself on that accumulation of sand and gravel washed by many tides and many storms into the southeast corner of the pier jutting under the East Cliff, known locally as Tate Hill Pier …

The scene is set for the arrival of the vampire in the disguise of a terrifying dog:

> But, strangest of all, the very instant the shore was touched, an immense dog sprang up on deck from below, as if shot up by the concussion, and running forward, jumped from the bow on the sand.
>
> Making straight for the steep cliff, where the churchyard hangs over the laneway to the East Pier so steeply that some of the flat tombstones, thruffsteans or through-stones, as they call them in Whitby vernacular, actually project over where the sustaining cliff has fallen away, it disappeared in the darkness, which seemed intensified just beyond the focus of the searchlight …
>
> A good deal of interest was abroad concerning the dog which landed when the ship struck, and more than a few of the members of the S.P.C.A., which is very strong in Whitby, have tried to befriend the animal. To the general disappointment, however, it was not to be found. It seems to have disappeared entirely from the town. It may be that it was frightened and made its way on to the moors, where it is still hiding in terror.
>
> There are some who look with dread on such a possibility, lest later on it should in itself become a danger, for it is evidently a fierce brute. Early this morning a large dog, a half-bred mastiff belonging to a coal

merchant close to Tate Hill Pier, was found dead in the roadway opposite its master's yard. It had been fighting, and manifestly had had a savage opponent, for its throat was torn away, and its belly was slit open as if with a savage claw.

An account, which has been regularly told, although the source is unknown, says that one night the howls of the Barguest echoed across the town. The next morning no one claimed to have heard the cry except for one man – it seemed that people were too frightened to get involved with any talk of the death hound, but they knew that the person who heard the howls was doomed. Sure enough, not long after hearing the dreaded cries of the beast, death carried the man away.

In his book, *Folk Tales from the North York Moors* (1990), Peter N. Walker tells of a man who was walking up a hill between Egton and Egton Bridge – about 7 miles from Whitby. The evening sky was getting darker when suddenly he was faced by a large, evil-looking black dog. The hound let out a ferocious howl and began to chase him. Whether it was a Barguest we do not know but his description was remarkably familiar – 'an awful creature … eyes like saucers.'

Could it be that the beast was real? If reports in the *Whitby Gazette* between 2006 and 2007 are anything to go by, a creature may still be out there – or at least an animal of a similar description. So frequent were the sightings of a large hound, the newspaper dubbed it the 'Beast of the Bay'. The *Whitby Gazette* even created an interactive map to show the places where the beast had been seen. Sightings were reported from all around the Whitby area, from Egton, Robin Hood's Bay, Fylingdales, Sleights and Runswick to Sneaton. What exactly is the 'Beast of the Bay'? The *Gazette* talked of a panther-like creature stalking the area around the abbey. Witnesses described the animal as 'jet black … large claws … awe-inspiring'. One witness said, 'I was shocked and a bit scared'; another claimed that 'lots of people have seen it but won't admit to it'.

The Gytrash of Goathland

The Gytrash is a spectral hound and a variation on the Barguest legend. It is a malevolent spirit that takes the form of a large dog, and leads people astray. There is a reference to the creature in Charlotte Brontë's *Jane Eyre*:

As this horse approached, and as I watched for it to appear through the dusk, I remembered certain of Bessie's tales, wherein figured a North-of-England spirit called a 'Gytrash,' which, in the form of horse, mule, or large dog, haunted solitary ways, and sometimes came upon belated travellers, as this horse was now coming upon me.

It was very near, but not yet in sight; when, in addition to the tramp, tramp, I heard a rush under the hedge, and close down by the hazel stems glided a great dog, whose black and white colour made him a distinct object against the trees. It was exactly one form of Bessie's Gytrash – a lion-like creature with long hair and a huge head … with strange pretercanine eyes … Nothing ever rode the Gytrash: it was always alone …

The local Gytrash legend centres around a small castle that was built on a site known as Julian Park on the road to Goathland. Julian de Mauley, who built the castle, was led to believe that if a living person or animal were locked up in the building, it would survive for all time. In order to fulfil this belief, de Mauley took an attractive young local woman called Gytha and, despite much opposition from her family and neighbours, incarcerated her within the walls of the new castle. As the final stones were laid around Gytha she was given water, bread, a spinning wheel and yards of yarn. She was then cruelly entombed within the walls. As the days past crying from the walls could be heard until all went quiet.

On the first anniversary of her entombment Julian was lying in his bed when he was suddenly shaken by the sound of loud and terrifying cries which gradually came closer. Frozen with fear his door slowly opened and there in a gown stood a white figure. It was the ghost of Gytha who was holding a spindle. Julian could only stare in absolute horror as she stood looking menacingly from the bottom of his bed. Gytha then proceeded to spin the yarn around his feet and then floated away. Paralysed, Julian could not move his feet.

Heartbeat country – Goathland from the Whitby to Pickering Road.

For the next ten years Gytha appeared on each anniversary to bind another part of Julian's body. In his desperation to redeem his sin he tried to do good works such as having a church built for the local community, but it was all to no avail. On the night of his death the fearful Gytrash appeared shortly after and brought with it great terror to people in the area. It was believed to be Julian who had turned into the beast.

Although Julian was now free to haunt the area, so was Gytha who began to weave her evil threads around young girls. If only Gytha could use her powers to get rid of the Gytrash. A trap was eventually laid to lure both of the spirits to the same place – the graveside of a fake dead baby. As the two antagonists moved across the moors they confronted each other at the graveside. Gytha wound her yarn around the Gytrash, who collapsed into the grave whilst Gytha disappeared into the night. Although both have long gone the sounds of wailing have been heard across the moors. Sceptics might say it is just the wind.

Other Animal Ghosts

What are these phantom hounds? Are they actually beasts roaming the countryside or are they really ghost dogs? If they are the latter, then this raises a long-held debate as to whether animals have souls and, if so, what type of soul? Can animals have ghosts? Historically, animals have been associated with shape shifting – as in the case of Dracula, or demons and witches. Pamphlets during the seventeenth century spoke of the Devil as appearing in 'diverse forms'. Animal apparitions have often been of a demonic nature as in the case of the Barguest or other local legends concerning black dogs. Witches were thought to have animal familiars – demons or imps who often appeared in the form of a small animal: cats, rabbits, toads and mice. These familiars were assumed to be the companions of a witch who would trade favours in return for milk from the witch's breast (a 'third teat'). In some cases, the familiar was believed to be the witch who changed shape to travel to the Sabbat – a midnight mass.

Some of the villages around Whitby had cases of women accused of practicing witchcraft which involved animals; for example, Ann Allan from Ugthorpe in 1780, Molly Milburn of Danby in 1663, Susan Ambler from Stokesley in 1699, Sabina Warters who was whipped in Leyburn in 1666, and a particular incident in Goathland. The latter, which involved two old women who annoyed their neighbours by assuming the form of cats, were accused of scratching at doors and running along the roofs.

These day sightings of such strange animals or large fearsome dogs have become more the object of curiosity or novelty rather than any association as the harbingers of doom. Although I have never seen such a beast I would prefer to be at a very safe distance from it!

A more recent case that involved the sighting of a strange animal was reported in the *Whitby Gazette* on 4 October 2006. A Sleights woman saw the mysterious creature in Sandsend, a short distance from Whitby. The woman was returning home while walking with her dog and a friend along Sandsend ravine on a stormy night at around 10.30 p.m. As they walked under the golf bridge she first caught sight of the animal which appeared to be enormous – some 4ft high and 3ft wide. The woman recalled that, 'The bottom of it seemed to have no legs'. The strange creature, which was next to a hedge, looked so unusually big that it made the couple stop in their tracks and they did not dare move. The creature just stared so the woman released her dog to investigate further. 'The dog … went racing up to see it off so it was obvious by her natural chasing instinct that this was some wild animal. As she approached it the odd thing was that there was no scuffle or running involved. The black thing seemed to glide sideways very gracefully and quietly like a ghost into the grass.'

The creature disappeared and was not reported again – well, not at Sandsend!

The Ghost of the Collie Dog

This account comes from 1931, when an old large house on the cliffs near Whitby was converted into a nursing home. A hundred years earlier a young girl had been found dead, possibly murdered, in one of the bedrooms. Her body was laid on one of the beds and immediately her devoted black and white collie dog lay across her body, refusing to move even for food or drink. Neither would it let anyone come near the body. The girl was eventually buried and the dog pined away and died shortly after.

By the early 1930s people had commented on hearing and even feeling the presence of a dog in that room. When a new nurse came to work at the home she was shown to the small wood-panelled room. She was advisedly told the story of the dog and how two nurses had left because they had been so scared by their experiences in the room. The nurse laughed and said that she did not believe in such things and was happy with her accommodation. On the first night that the woman slept in the room she was disturbed by what she described as a suffocating experience. She shrugged this off, but on the second night she felt the same sensation. It was as if a large heavy dog was lying on top of her. She complained and requested another room. Despite her earlier scepticism she was not prepared to continue sleeping with the unexplained visitor.

A version of this story, in W.R. Mitchell's *Haunted Yorkshire* (1969), has added a further twist. After the nurse complained about the room an investigation took place. A passage was found behind a grilled ventilator which had been fitted to the foot of one of the wood panels. The passage had steps that led to a cave at the foot of the cliff. The discovery also offered an explanation as to the suffocating effect experienced by various individuals. As the tide filled the cave air was being pushed up the passage and it apparently compressed the bedroom. Additional ventilation was added to the bedroom and there were no more reports of the 'ghost dog'.

MUTILATED GHOSTS

Is the sight of a ghost reassuring, comforting or terrifying? When someone looks pale and shocked, it is said that they look as though they have seen a ghost. Even the Bible makes this point when Eliphaz answers:

> Fear came upon me, and trembling, which made all my bones to shake.
> Then a spirit passed before my face; the hair of my flesh stood up:
> It stood still, but I could not discern the form thereof: an image was before mine eyes, there was silence …
> (Job 4:14-16)

Fear might depend on the context in which an apparition is seen or the type of spirit that presents itself. For example, there are many stories of headless ghosts throughout Britain and Europe, although most accounts of such sightings in England come mainly from the seventeenth century with few, if any, recordings during the medieval period. Why headless? An obvious answer is that it is the ghost of someone who had suffered a beheading via execution (although these were much less common than hangings) or, as in the case of King Edwin whose body came to rest in Whitby Abbey, a head lost in battle. A headless condition may also be the result of some unfortunate accident. Whitby historian Revd J.C. Atkinson recalled knowing of the headless ghost of a blood-stained Essex woman when he lived there as a child.

In his book *Haunted: A Social History of Ghosts* (2007), Owen Davies suggests that headless ghosts can be partly explained in terms of Christian ideas about the fate of mutilated bodies at the Day of Judgement. Would God restore any missing body part in the afterlife? The answer was notably reassuring and claimed that the 'resurrected body would be identical to the complete body with its soul'. Despite all this, the sightings of headless ghosts are actually rare in first-hand experiences and they tend to be based more on legend. Bearing in mind that we have mentioned the spectre at the abbey who frightened the treasure hunters, and the fact that King Edwin's decapitated body was buried at the abbey, Whitby has a few stories involving headless ghosts as well as a macabre tale of a decapitated hand.

Seven

FUNERAL COACH AND HORSES

A well-known story told over many years is that of a headless ghost (some accounts suggest it is not headless) who drives a coach-like funeral hearse pulled by black horses which races over the cliffs near the abbey and into the sea. The story varies in its telling but one account states that when a Whitby sailor was buried, a large hearse with four jet-black horses would appear beside the grave at night ready to take the sailor away. A group of ghostly mourners would appear from the coach and remove the body from its grave. The coach, lit by burning torches and driven by a phantom coachman shrouded in a black cloak, would then gallop away at speed. It would hurtle from the churchyard, turn into Henrietta Street and then drive frantically towards the cliff top and leap into the sea, carrying the sailor to his watery grave.

East Cliff where the phantom coach and horses plunge over the edge into the sea.

Eight

BAGDALE HALL

The headless ghost which haunts Bagdale Hall is believed to be one its previous owners, Browne Bushell (1609-1651). Bushell was born at Ruswarp in May 1609. He later married the daughter of Sir Thomas Fairfax (1612-1671), Chief of Staff of the Parliamentary forces. Bushell, who was a frequent turncoat, became captain in the Parliamentary forces during the Civil War and in 1645 he was given command of a ship in the Parliamentary Navy.

He had been responsible for the betrayal of the Royalist-held Scarborough Castle and in yet another about-turn he allowed the castle to be handed back to the Royalists, for which he was placed under arrest by his father-in-law. Although he was court-martialled in 1645, he was found not guilty and rejoined the Parliamentary forces.

Three years later, in 1648, he committed another act of betrayal. Bushell was one of a number of captains who delivered their ships to the Prince of Wales. For this he was arrested and sent to Windsor where he spent the next two years. The *House of Commons Journal* (April 1648) declared that, 'Captain Browne Bushell be committed to the Castle of Windsore', where he was to be kept safe in prison. It later added that 'the Committee of the Admiralty do consider of a speedy Course for the Tryal of Browne Bushell, for his Piracy, and other Crimes'. Bushell, who was beheaded on 29 March 1651, was one of three people executed on Tower Hill that year.

The plaque dedicated to Browne Bushell, who reputedly haunts the hall.

Bagdale Hall, built originally in the sixteenth century but underwent extensive changes in the nineteenth century.

Bagdale Hall was built in 1516 for the Conyers, an important Whitby family, until the Bushells, who were prosperous merchants and ship owners, took it over in 1595. Browne Bushell inherited the estate from his father Nicholas. Over the years it has had different owners until, in the nineteenth century, it underwent extensive restoration which changed its features substantially from its original appearance. Whitby historian Percy Shaw Jeffrey bought the house in 1914. It is now Bagdale Hall Hotel and is situated in a quieter corner near the centre of Whitby, close to the railway station.

In addition to appearances of the headless ghost of Browne Bushell walking up the staircase, there have also been a number of other strange experiences at the Hall which include the sighting of an apparition, the noise of distinctive footsteps walking around the house, unexplained noises from the kitchen and the sounds of children playing just after midnight in empty rooms. Cecelia Hunter and Paul Pearson (*The Ghosts of Bagdale Hall*, Whitby Archive Heritage Centre) note the various encounters of people with ghosts at the Hall. For example, a maid recalled on one occasion how a duster flew out of her hand and in the direction of the kitchen whilst she was cleaning the library. When the maid told Percy Shaw Jeffrey, he replied that such events happened frequently. In fact, a local photographer witnessed poltergeist activity during Jeffrey's occupancy. Frightened by crockery flying from a cabinet, the photographer looked in the direction of the stairs where he saw the fleeting figure of a woman in white quickly dissolve away.

In another incident a former chef asked a waitress why an old gentleman in the restaurant was not being served. Her response was that there was no one in the dining room. When the chef returned to check, sure enough, there was nobody there despite the fact that he had clearly seen someone.

Many of the past owners of the Hall, as well as staff working there, have reported cases of unexplained sightings, noises and the inexplicable movement of physical objects.

Nine

HANNAH GRUNDY

A very different type of headless ghost story concerns Hannah Grundy, a young Staithes girl who once gathered bait for fishermen in the early nineteenth century. Whilst men in fishing communities generally caught the fish, the women played an essential role in preparing the catches for the fishery at places such as the Whitby quayside stalls or around the town. The women would also be involved in processing, distributing and disposing the catch as well as collecting bait. In addition to their work they raised children who would also contribute to the needs of the fishing community. The women's work was often low paid and irregular. Women and young girls in fishing villages around Whitby such as Staithes, Runswick Bay and Robin Hood's Bay had to search out 'flithers' for bait. These would be found around the rocks and could mean walking up to 20 miles to find supplies. Younger, unmarried women generally did such work.

In 1807 Hannah was out gathering bait along with three other girls when she decided to stop for a rest at the side of a steep cliff. Little did she know that the rest would prove to be so fateful. Shortly after she had sat down, a large stone fell down from the cliff and sliced off her head. It was a tragic and gruesome way to die. Not long after her death sightings of a transparent, headless, waif-like figure was seen wandering along the sea front as if looking at the stones. The sightings continued for years and were seen mainly during the month of April.

Since at least 1905 and even more recently, people have reported seeing a haunting, 'mysterious white wraith' along the area of West Cliff beach at Whitby. It has been described as an almost transparent 'apparition floating down the face of the cliff'. It is uncertain whether this apparition has any association with Hannah.

Ten

THE HAND OF GLORY

Probably the most popular exhibit in Whitby Museum is a macabre and sinister hand. The 'Hand of Glory' was supposedly cut from the body of an executed criminal while the corpse was still hanging from the gibbet. It was then subjected to a particular preserving process that involved the blood being squeezed out of the hand. It was then embalmed in a shroud and steeped in a solution of saltpetre, salt and pepper (herbs and horse dung might be included) and then dried for two weeks in an oven. Robbers who used the hand when breaking into buildings and homes used it as a charm.

However, before the preservation ritual was complete, there was another task to be performed. It was essential that a candle should be made, preferably from a hanged man's fat (the wick being made from his

Hand of Glory. The original can be seen in Whitby Museum.

hair), wax and Lapland sesame. The candle would then be fixed between the fingers of the hand and then lit when the burglar broke into a house. A less-demanding method of curing the severed and dried hand was to dip it in wax and this would allow the fingers themselves to be lit. Why all this elaborate ritual? The hand was supposed to open locks, make the thief invisible, and send the household into a deep sleep. Once equipped with the hand and the candle, a charm was then spoken along the lines of 'Hand of Glory, Hand of Glory, let those who are asleep remain asleep – in a sleep that is fast and deep! But those who are awake be wide-awake!' The only way the spell could be broken was by putting out the flames with blood or skimmed milk. Once this was done the household could then be awakened.

How could unsuspecting householders prevent such a spell from being used? There were some remedies such as the use of various types of ointments, including the blood of screech owls or the fat of a white hen which was smeared around the doorway to keep the intruder away.

During the sixteenth and seventeenth centuries the Hand of Glory was believed to be used in witchcraft rituals. For example, in cases in Germany and Scotland people accused of witchcraft often confessed to using Hands of Glory to light their way in graveyards in order to perform either the exhumation of bodies or to carry out a ceremony to the Devil. As in many witchcraft cases, these 'confessions' said more about those extracting the admission under torture than what the accused witch actually did.

The Hand of Glory in Whitby Museum, which was reputedly found in the attic of a house in Eskdale, is a unique exhibit. There is a Hand of Glory on display in Walsall Museum (actually an arm and a hand) that was discovered hidden up a chimney during building work on the White Hart Inn in the 1870s, but it is that of a child which was preserved with formalin.

There are many references to the Hand of Glory in literature and film, including *The Wicker Man*, *Harry Potter and the Chamber of Secrets*, and *Harry Potter and the Half Blood Prince*.

Eleven

THE LAST HOUSE AT RUNSWICK BAY

Erosion always threatens the coastline. A tragedy with a rather eerie twist took place in 1682, when the original village of Runswick Bay slid into the sea as a result of a landslip. The incident happened on a day when most of the locals were attending a wake at the house of a deceased person. Fortunately for them a guest who had arrived late noticed the steps to the house slipping away under his feet. He quickly alerted the mourners who all looked outside to see what was happening. To their alarm they saw the ground sliding several feet down the cliff. They quickly fled from the building and warned the rest of the village, who managed to run to safety. The next morning every house had fallen into the sea with the exception of one – the house of the dead man. Although the village was rebuilt the land was still fragile and another landslip caused the destruction of cottages in December 1872.

The attractive haven of Runswick Bay.

Twelve

DRACULA

The story of Dracula exerts its haunting influence over many parts of Whitby. The author of the Gothic horror novel *Dracula*, Abraham 'Bram' Stoker (1847-1912), was born in Dublin. He moved to London in 1876 to manage the Lyceum Theatre as well as the famous actor Sir Henry Irving. Whilst in England Stoker visited Whitby, where he took many holidays. Although he had started working on *Dracula* in March 1890 before he came to Whitby, the town provided rich material for the book. Many myths have grown up around the writing of the book and who the characters were based on. Elizabeth Miller, writing in *Dracula: Sense and Nonsense* (2006), dispels some of the 'mistaken assumptions' and states that 'during the past thirty years, we have been bombarded with a plethora of significant errors and misconceptions about Stoker and his famous novel'. She adds that:

> The single most important resource for anyone researching the writing of *Dracula* is Stoker's working notes for the novel. Housed at the Rosenbach Museum in Philadelphia, 'Bram Stoker's Original Foundation Notes & Data for his *Dracula*' comprise both handwritten and typewritten notes. These include early plans for the book, chapter outlines, a list of characteristics of vampires, several pages of notes taken at Whitby, an article entitled 'Vampires in New England' and numerous jottings which Stoker made from crucial source books. Also useful are comments that he made himself in a newspaper interview shortly after the novel was published.

Whitby proved an inspirational setting for the novel for several reasons. An important piece of information from the notes mentioned above indicates where Stoker found the name 'Dracula.' Whilst in Whitby during the summer of 1890, he came across a book in the public library titled *An Account of the Principalities of Wallachia and Moldavia* (1820) by William Wilkinson. From this book he learned that there had been a Wallachian ruler in the fifteenth century nicknamed Dracula, who had fought against the Turks with some brief success. Stoker highlighted in the notes a footnote referring to the comment made by Wilkinson that, 'Dracula in the Wallachian language means Devil'. The actual title of Stoker's classic book until 1897 was to be 'The Un-Dead', and the decision to change it to Dracula was made virtually at the last minute.

The haunting atmosphere of the town captivated Stoker. The ruins of the abbey and the tales he heard from local fishermen all influenced his masterpiece. It was not the first novel to deal with vampires, and Stoker's book did not receive a great deal of acclaim when it was first published. Nonetheless, it would become enormously successful and grip the public imagination in later years.

Historian P.G. Maxwell Stuart, in his book *Ghosts* (Tempus, 2006), tells us that the English word 'vampire' was first used in The *London Journal* in March 1732 to report the dreadful discovery that dead bodies in Hungary had been killing people by sucking their blood. This sparked many debates about vampires, which then fuelled a great deal of writing and scholarship about the subject. Stoker was probably aware of the growing literature on the topic. Shortly after the publication of the book, Stoker gave an interview in July 1897 to the *British Weekly*. He was asked if there was any historical basis for the legend. His reply was:

> It rested, I imagine, on some such case as this. A person may have fallen into a death-like trance and been buried before the time. Afterwards the body may have been dug up and found alive, and from this a horror seized upon

Bram Stoker.

the people, and in their ignorance they imagined that a vampire was about. The more hysterical, through excess of fear, might themselves fall into trances in the same way; and so the story grew that one vampire might enslave many others and make them like himself. Even in the single villages it was believed that there might be many such creatures. When once the panic seized the population, their only thought was to escape.

(Reprinted in *Dracula* (1998) by Glennis Byron)

The belief in the un-dead goes back much earlier. William of Newburgh (which is on the edge of the North York Moors) wrote in the late twelfth century that, 'It would not be easy to believe that the corpses of the dead should sally from their graves, and should wander about to the terror or destruction of the living, and again return to the tomb …' In one particular case he described the way in which a corpse was dug up from its grave and dragged to the village where a funeral pile was constructed. 'The pestilential body would not burn unless its heart were torn out.' Once removed, 'the body [was] now consigned to the flames … When that infernal hell-hound had thus been destroyed, the pestilence which was rife among the people ceased, as if the air, which had been corrupted by the contagious motions of the dreadful corpse, were already purified by the fire which had consumed it.'

Another important event in Whitby that helped to inform Dracula was the ship *Demeter*, in which Dracula arrived in the shape of a black dog. His arrival at Tate Hill Pier was based on the shipwreck of the *Dmitri*, a Russian ship from the port of Narva, which ran aground at Whitby on 24 October 1885. The archives of the *Whitby Gazette* furnished Stoker with some of the details: 'The Russian schooner *Dmitri* of Navra … came in suddenly, in heavy weather, but going ashore in "Collier's Hope" became a total wreck.' Stoker heard macabre tales from the local fishermen, and, in her biography of Stoker, Barbara Belford writes how he first heard an account of the ship whilst on a visit to the lighthouse at Whitby:

The piers and cliffs were thronged with expectant people, when a few hundred yards from the piers she was knocked about considerably by the heavy seas, but on crossing the bar the sea calmed a little and she sailed into smooth water. A cheer broke from the spectators on the pier when they saw her into safety.

(*Bram Stoker: A Biography of the Author of Dracula*, Weidenfeld & Nicolson, 1996, p. 222)

The first mention of Whitby in Dracula comes in chapter two in Jonathan Harker's Journal. Harker is a solicitor employed in purchasing a property in England for Dracula. When Dracula leaves the room

The west lighthouse, harbour and sea.

in his castle Harker looks at some books around him and sees an atlas. 'On looking at it I found in certain places little rings marked, and on examining these I noticed that one was near London on the east side, manifestly where his new estate was situated. The other two were Exeter, and Whitby on the Yorkshire coast.'

Stoker's book returns to Whitby in chapter six. Mina Murray, Harker's fiancée and a schoolmistress, keeps a journal where she records that:

> Lucy [Lucy Westenra, Mina's best friend] met me at the station, looking sweeter and lovelier than ever, and we drove up to the house at the Crescent in which they have rooms [the Royal Crescent Street in Whitby – Stoker stayed in a house on the West Cliff]. Mina describes the town as a lovely place. The little river, the Esk, runs through a deep valley, which broadens out as it comes near the harbour. A great viaduct runs across, with high piers, through which the view seems somehow further away than it really is. The valley is beautifully green, and it is so steep that when you are on the high land on either side you look right across it, unless you are near enough to see down. The houses of the old town – the side away from us, are all red-roofed … Whitby Abbey … is a most noble ruin, of immense size, and full of beautiful and romantic bits.

She writes about the parish church and the 'big graveyard' and the many graves, 'mostly of sandstone which have been weathered for hundreds of years … some of the graves have been destroyed'. Stoker had visited St Mary's Churchyard and it was from one of the inscriptions on a tombstone that he took the name of Mr Swales. In the book Swales is an old local man who is full of provincial wisdom but who dies during the dreadful storm. There were a number of Swales in and around Whitby at this time. A cursory search shows, for example, an Isaac Swales aged twenty, listed as a master mariner from the 1851 census and George Swales of Burns Yard, Flowergate, who was a jet worker in Whitby in 1899. A much earlier but interesting coincidence is that of Christopher Swales, a blacksmith, who, in January 1809, was reported as one of several persons who 'lost their lives' in a storm whilst 'attempting to return home from Whitby market.'

Old Mr Swales told tales of local legend, history and ghost stories of Whitby which stood in stark contrast to Transylvania. The Whitby ghosts, such as those associated with the abbey, are eerie, but they don't compare to the evil that lurked in Transylvania and which preyed on the living. Even Whitby's graveyard is more genteel and does not frighten the locals, unlike Transylvania where the peasants lived in fear and, as Jonathan Harker wrote, 'where the Devil and his children still walk with earthly feet.'

Days later and worrying that she has heard nothing from Jonathan Harker, Mina reflects on what was to be a foreboding:

The houses of the old town are all red-roofed.

The graveyard by St Mary's Church.

Last night was very threatening, and the fishermen say that we are in for a storm ... the sea ... sounds like some passage of doom ... The fishing boats are racing for home, and rise and dip in the ground swell as they sweep into the harbour. Old Mr Swales confirms the terror that is getting nearer: There's something in that wind ... that sounds, and looks, and tastes, and smells like death. It's in the air. I feel it comin'.

The coastguard then sights a strange ship. 'I can't make her out', he said. 'She's a Russian, by the look of her ... She seems to see the storm coming, but can't decide whether to run up north in the open, or to put in here.'

Tate Hill Pier where the ship that brought Dracula, the *Demeter*, came ashore.

Looking over Robin Hood's Bay.

Chapter seven deals with the arrival of Dracula in Whitby. Mina pasted a cutting from The *Dailygraph* in her journal recording the storm that hit Whitby in the month of August. It reported that holidaymakers had been going about their …

> … visits to Mulgrave Woods, Robin Hood's Bay, Rig Mill, Runswick, Staithes, and the various trips in the neighborhood of Whitby. The steamers *Emma* and *Scarborough* made trips up and down the coast, and there was an unusual amount of 'tripping' both to and from Whitby. However, before midnight there came a strange sound from over the sea … Then without warning the tempest broke. The huge cashing waves broke

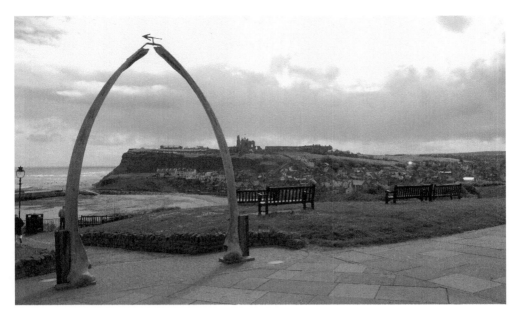

View from West Cliff, where Mina looked out towards the graveyard to see her friend Lucy fall victim to Dracula.

over the piers, and with their spume swept the lanthorns of the lighthouses which rise from the end of either pier of Whitby Harbour.

The *Demeter* was seen struggling in the storm:

> … and there was a shudder amongst the watchers on the cliff as they realized the terrible danger in which she was now was. There was a greater shudder when the spectators saw what was lashed to the helm: a corpse, with drooping head, which swung horribly to and fro at each motion of the ship. As the ship crashed onto the sand an immense dog sprang up on deck from below, as if shot up by the concussion, and running forward, jumped from the bow on the sand. It quickly made for the steep cliff, where the churchyard hangs over the laneway to the East Pier.

Dracula had arrived.

Apart from some occasional references to Whitby recalling what had happened there, the story moves away from the town. Clearly Whitby had a huge influence on Stoker in the writing of this classic Gothic horror. Not only did he glean information from the pubic library (which was then near the quayside) and the local paper, but he also drew on stories associated with Whitby: the wreck of the ship which he called *Demeter*, the ghosts of the abbey, maritime tales, the black dog and the black coach drawn by black horses (which was driven by Dracula in Transylvania). In addition, there are descriptions of many parts of the town, particularly from Mina Murray's journal at the beginning of chapter six, which almost resembles something from a tourist promotion brochure for Whitby.

Whitby celebrates its connection with Stoker and Dracula through the Whitby Dracula Society, the Dracula Experience on Marine Parade, the Dracula Walks and a memorial bench on the cliff top path which is inscribed with the words:

> The view from this spot inspired Bram Stoker (1847-1912) to use Whitby as the setting of part of his world-famous novel DRACULA. This seat was erected by Scarborough Borough Council and the Dracula Society to mark the 68th Anniversary of Stoker's death – April 20th 1980.

Thirteen

THE HAUNTED LIGHTHOUSE

The present lighthouses on the pier appeared in Whitby in the nineteenth century. *The History and Topography of the City of York*, and the *North Riding of Yorkshire*, published five years after the completion of the second lighthouse, commented that the 'handsome lighthouse which stands at the head of the west pier was erected in 1831, and is a fine fluted Doric column, 75 feet high. On the head of the east pier a second lighthouse was erected in 1854 and is 40 feet high'. In *Dracula*, Mina Murray commented that:

> The harbour lies below me, with, on the far side, one long granite wall stretching out into the sea, with a curve outwards at the end of it, in the middle of which is a lighthouse. A heavy seawall runs along outside of it. On the near side, the seawall makes an elbow crooked inversely, and its end too has a lighthouse.

There is a ghost story associated with the lighthouse on the west pier, concerning a young girl in the 1950s who saw the ghost of an old harbour man who died of a heart attack. As the girl climbed the stairs with her mother she complained that she could not get past the 'old man' lying in her way. When her mother looked no one was there. However, there is also a strange story concerning another lighthouse further south.

The Whitby lighthouse near Whitestone Point is over a mile south of the town on Ling Hill. It is sometimes referred to as the 'Whitby Bull' because of the foghorn that can be heard miles away. Trinity House, which built the lighthouse, was chartered in 1514 by Henry VIII and has operated lighthouses in Britain for nearly 500 years. The one near Whitby was designed by James Walker and was originally a pair of towers, aligned north-south and showing fixed lights over Whitby Rock. The station was altered in 1890 when a more efficient light was installed in the smaller tower and the other closed down. It was automated in 1992 and is monitored and controlled via telemetry link from the Trinity House Operations Control Centre at Harwich. The *Guardian* newspaper in November 2006 described the lighthouse as a 'great big white punctuation mark at the end of the road. It's spooky and dramatic, yet reassuring.'

A close friend told me of a strange incident he experienced whilst walking the popular and beautiful coastal route between Robin Hood's Bay and Whitby in 1988. By late afternoon he and his partner saw the lighthouse in the distance as they approached it. Suddenly, as if out of nowhere, a man appeared carrying what seemed to be a box supported on one shoulder. The box must have contained fish given its shape and the interest shown by a large flock of seagulls hovering above. Both my friend and his partner said that there was something very unreal about the man who looked eerie. In fact, the whole atmosphere became uncomfortable. Having known this friend for over twenty years, he is certainly not one for believing too easily in ghosts or the supernatural. He is a very sceptical person.

Nonetheless, he and his partner obviously thought that the man with the fish had come from the beach, but as they looked towards him there was something not right at all. He walked in a strange manner, almost floating, and although he appeared to be walking slowly they could not catch up with him despite quickening their pace in order to get a closer look. The man headed towards the lighthouse and then, as though dissolving into thin air, he and the seagulls disappeared from sight. The reason this incident stayed with him is because of his natural inclination to disbelieve and the fact that he could not explain the strange event.

Fourteen

THE CREEPY TUNNEL

On the West Cliff near to Khyber Pass is a small passage that leads to steps that descend towards the harbour. The view through the passage towards the town offers a picturesque framed image of the abbey. The passage has been variously referred to as the Screaming Tunnel, Dracula's Tunnel and Hudson's Tunnel. Any tunnel, no matter how long or short, is creepy at night or even in the day.

There are many tales concerning this particular tunnel and caution is offered about walking through the passage at night. Various accounts have spoken of an eerie atmosphere or of feelings of not being alone. A middle-aged couple taking a holiday in Whitby in 2006 recalled walking into town from their hotel at East Crescent via the tunnel. It was a walk they had taken a few times during their stay and they had often commented about the creepiness of it. The creepiness became a reality on the next two occasions that they took their regular walk through the passage. On the first occasion, the woman was taken aback to see what she thought was the dark figure, a man standing at the end of the passage. When she told her husband he dismissed it and said it was probably someone in front of them also taking a walk. When they reached the other side there was no sign of anyone. The following evening they were returning from town to the hotel and it was late and dark. As they walked through the passage the husband felt his wife take a firm grasp of his hand for reassurance. The man laughed and asked if she could see any dark figures. His wife said, 'Sorry what did you say?' He looked around and his wife was walking a few steps behind him. She could not possibly have been holding his hand.

Another Creepy Tunnel

Sandsend railway station was part of the Whitby, Redcar and Middlesbrough Union Railway (WRMU) which was taken over by North Eastern Railway in 1889. The railway was built in the 1880s but closed in 1958 and the track was dismantled in the early 1960s. Part of this track included the Sansdend Rail Tunnel. The old, disused tunnel runs to Kettleness and is nearly a mile in length. The entrance gives a rather creepy invitation to look inside. Once inside any fears that one might have had are confirmed by the gloominess of the long, dark tunnel. Needless to say there are rumours that the tunnel is haunted. A number of people have reported seeing white lights or figures passing through the walls. Some have heard the sound of a whistle from a steam train and the sound of footsteps.

Fifteen

SHIPWRECKS

The sea around Britain's coastline has been the grave to thousands of unfortunate souls. In fact, most shipwreck ghost stories come from the British Isles. Shipwrecks certainly provided rich pickings for the locals. George Young, in his *History of Whitby*, noted how the 'numbers among the lower orders in Whitby discover a shameful propensity to pilfering'. He added, 'I have seen Whitby vomiting forth its inhabitants, by scores if not hundreds, to share in the spoils of a shipwreck, even on the Lord's Day'.

The coast around Whitby has had its fair share of disasters, particularly the loss of the Whitby Lifeboat on 12 February 1861 which was victim to a terrible storm. With several thousand people looking on they heard the 'fearful agonies of those powerful men, buffeting with the fury of the breakers, till one by one 12 out of 13 sank, and only one survived' (letter to *The Times* from William Keane, Curate of Whitby). The worst tragedy was that of the *Rohilla* on Halloween, 31 October 1914, which in a violent storm claimed the lives of eight-four people.

In another book of mine, *Haunted London Underground*, I wrote about the tragedy at the Bethnal Green tube station in which 173 people were crushed to death in 1943 – the single worst civilian disaster of the Second World War. Over the years there have been a number of accounts from workers on the Underground hearing the screams and cries of women and children (they were the majority of the victims) from that station. Attempts to explain the noises have suggested they are caused variously by the wind, people above ground and the extent of infrasound. Infrasound is sound with a frequency too low to be heard by the human ear and has often been used to monitor earthquakes. It is known to cause feelings of sickness but, as it is not consciously perceived, it can make people feel they are experiencing supernatural events. The distortion of sound might be offered to explain the reports of strange noises heard on cliff tops. The noise could be a combination of the wind and the sea, although people have described hearing distinctive screams of drowning men off the coast where the *Rohilla* sank.

It was on 29 October 1914 that the 7,400-ton naval hospital ship *Rohilla* left Queensferry for Dunkirk on her last voyage with 229 people on board. During the early hours of 30 October she ran onto the rocks at Saltwick Nab, about a mile south of Whitby. The weather was so bad that it was impossible to send out the Whitby Lifeboat. Instead, the *John Fielden*, which was kept afloat in the harbour, was launched at 7 a.m. It managed to fight its way through the awful conditions and rescued twelve men and five nurses. However, after rescuing eighteen men on the second trip, the *John Fielden* was damaged and could not go out again.

Eventually, the Scarborough Lifeboat *Queensbury*, towed by a steam trawler, arrived at Saltwick Nab at 6 p.m. in the dark, destructive weather. Any attempt at rescue was impossible despite waiting eighteen hours. Other boats tried to help including Teesmouth Lifeboat *Bradford IV*, the *Robert & Mary Ellis* of Whitby and the Upgang Lifeboat *William Riley*. By 4.15 p.m. on that fateful 31 October, the *Henry Vernon* from Tynemouth was called upon. During the night and early morning some forty men were brought aboard the lifeboat before it and the *Rohilla* were hit by two huge waves, but even then a further ten people were rescued. Despite the tragic loss of life, 145 out of the 229 crew, doctors and nurses survived, making it the greatest rescue off the Whitby coast. The bodies of those who died were washed ashore

This Monument

WAS ERECTED BY THE BRITISH INDIA
STEAM NAVIGATION COMPANY LTD
OWNERS OF THE HOSPITAL SHIP S.S.
"ROHILLA", TO THE MEMORY OF
31 OFFICERS AND MEN, WHO WERE
DROWNED IN THE WRECK OF THAT VESSEL
OFF WHITBY, OCTOBER 30TH 1914.
THIRTY THREE BODIES RECOVERED
FROM THE WRECK ARE BURIED HERE
THE NAMES OF FOURTEEN OF THOSE
IDENTIFIED ARE AS FOLLOW:-

A. PAGE.
S. MORRIS.
D. NISBET.
E. ROSE.
J. SMITH.
L. NICHOLSON.
R. GLOVER.
J. HARE.
J. G. ROSS.
H. W. WEATHERSTONE.
D. PATON.
M. TARBET.
W. BARRON.
J. PATON.

I SAW A NEW HEAVEN AND A NEW EARTH,
AND THERE WAS NO MORE SEA.

The memorial in Whitby Cemetery to those who perished on the *Rohilla*.

and collected by the townsfolk. Many of the crewmen were buried at Whitby cemetery where there is a commemoration stone dedicated to them. However, there are also many bodies that were never recovered. Some locals have said how they have seen ghostly figures on gloomy nights on the stretch of coast where the ship hit the rocks.

Sixteen

WRAITHS

To see your double walking towards you would be something of a shock to the system. If you were aware of the significance of this phenomenon there would be good cause to be terrified because you would have witnessed your own wraith – a portent of death. It is believed the word was first used in 1513 to mean ghost or spirit, but over time it has other associations, particularly in the twentieth century where writers from Tolkien to Rowling have used the term, as well as a host of films and games. A wraith, however, is generally considered to be the reflected image of a person seen immediately before death, as if it were a premonition of the Grim Reaper figure.

Wraiths (or autophany, which means seeing one's double) have had various names, including fetch, waff, fye, swarth and taff, but they are usually taken to be doubles that also act as death omens. The double may appear real, or have a filmy, ghostly look. It may also manifest itself in other ways, such as in the reflection in a window or a mirror or as a shadow. The belief in the idea of seeing one's double is based on the notion that an important part of an individual, such as their psyche, soul, spectral or astral form, may become detached wholly or in part from their body, thus leading to a temporary independent existence.

Queen Elizabeth I (reign 1558-1603) saw herself as a wraith. A figure had come to warn the queen of her approaching end. Wraiths have made themselves visible to close friends or relatives of the person who is about to die. The poet John Dunne (1572-1631), whilst in Paris, saw a wraith of his wife. She appeared before him holding their dead child in her arms at the very moment she was actually delivering it stillborn back in England. The poet Percy Shelley (1792-1822) saw his double pointing him towards the sea where he was soon to meet his death by drowning.

The belief that the soul exists in a visible double is ancient and widespread. William Henderson offered a number of examples of wraiths in Yorkshire and the north of England in *Folklore of the Northern Counties* (1866). Acknowledging that there were many omens of death from the croaking of a raven, the howling of dogs at night or the sight of a solitary magpie, he stressed that the most fatal of all was for someone to see their own wraith walking towards them at noon or before sunset. He tells a story passed on to him by a highly respectable old man of eighty-two from Danby, some 15 miles from Whitby. Years earlier the man was passing his uncle's home one evening when he saw the glow of firelight through the window. Curious as to why a fire might be burning, given that his uncle 'had long been bed-fast in the room above', he looked through the window. To his absolute surprise he saw his uncle seated in what used to be his favourite chair. There was no doubt about what he saw, 'the form and features were those of his relation'. The man entered the house in hope of greeting his uncle but when he stepped into the room it was dark, the seat was empty and the old man not there. He was still lying in his bed upstairs. Shortly after this incident the man's uncle died.

Another sighting of a wraith involved a tradesman from Whitby who was suffering from a failing kidney. He had been ordered to go into hospital at York to undergo an operation. Before he set out on his journey he experienced his double, his own wraith, the harbinger of doom. The man said there was no point in attending the operation because he knew he would die during the operation or immediately after it. Nonetheless, he was persuaded to go to York and he reluctantly went ahead with his operation. Tragically, he was proved right because he died soon after surgery.

St Mary's Church, Scarborough.

A particularly eerie account of a wraith took place on the Eve of St Mark (24 April) in the late eighteenth century. From the seventeenth to the late nineteenth century, it was the custom in villages in England on St Mark's Eve to sit in the church porch for an hour both sides of midnight for three successive years. At the third sitting, according to custom, the wraiths of those who were to die during the next twelve months passed in grim and ghostly procession into the church. Variations of this tradition have suggested that those watching would see headless or rotting corpses, or coffins entering the church. William Henderson gives an account of a particular experience that took place on the Eve of St Mark at Scarborough in the 1780s when parishioners gathered in the church porch of St Mary's. One of the watchers was an old woman who looked at the line of figures who slowly and sombrely walked and turned their faces towards her. Suddenly she was taken aback as one of the ghostly parade stopped and stared at her. The woman looked back with horror. It was her double. The women screamed and fell senseless to the ground. Neighbours took her back to their house but the shock of what she had seen was too much for her and she died shortly after.

Percy Shaw Jeffrey acknowledged the custom of watching on the Eve of St Mark in Whitby. Before the old Norman parish church was pulled down, towards the end of the eighteenth century it was customary for Whitby folk to gather in this porch on the vigil of St Mark, when on the stroke of midnight shadowy forms might be seen passing through on their way from the church to the churchyard.

The poet James Montgomery (1771-1854), who lived in various parts of Yorkshire, summed up the whole idea of the custom in this extract from *The Vigil of St Mark*:

''T'is now', replied the village belle,
St Mark's mysterious Eve;
'And all that old traditions tell
I tremblingly believe –

How when the midnight signal tolls
Along the churchyard green
A mournful train of sentenced souls
In winding-sheets are seen

The ghosts of all whom death shall doom
Within this coming year,
In pale procession walk the gloom,
Amid the silence drear.'

Twenty years after William Henderson gave his accounts of wraiths in the northern counties, prominent members of the Society for Physical Research in the late nineteenth century gave particular importance to the subject of wraiths. Frank Podmore (1856-1910), Frederic W.H. Myers (1843-1901) and Edmund Gurney (1847-1888) argued in their two-volume book, *Phantasms of the Living* (1886), that ghosts were not the souls of the dead returning to earth. This radical view caused splits in the membership of the society and many left. Gurney, Myers and Podmore believed that they had found evidence for the reality of wraiths. In fact, they maintained that there were many more wraiths than ghosts. Their view was that after death the body went through a process of dissolution in which it retained some psychic energy.

In 1988 a nurse told me of an experience she had which has a bearing on this view. She was working on a night shift looking after a ward where people were either critical or approaching death. As she went in to check on the patients she saw what could only be described as many small bright lights hovering 2–3ft above one of the patient's bed. She went to check on him, but he had just died.

Can anything be done to stop the impending doom following the sighting of one's own wraith? Eliza Gutch (1840-1931) in her book *Examples of Printed Folk-lore Concerning the North Riding of Yorkshire* (1901) offered one particular solution: If anyone sees his own waff, 'he can avert his fate by speaking to it severely'. She gives an example of a native of Guisborough who, on going into a shop at Whitby, saw his own waff looking back at him. He addressed it boldly: 'What's thou doin' here? What's thou doin' here? Thou's after no good … Get thy ways yom with thee! Get thy ways yom!' It is said that the 'waff' slowly sidled away, feeling rather ashamed. The man apparently had no further trouble with it. It would appear that the combination of Yorkshire stubbornness and bluntness worked in this case.

Seventeen

HOBS

For a generation of people who saw the BBC series *Quatermass and the Pit* in the late 1950s, the term hob had very scary and evil associations. In one of the episodes it was said that hob was an old name for the Devil. However, the type of hob in *Quatermass* was very different to those which are said to haunt the byways of Whitby. Nonetheless, the Yorkshire hobs could be very mischievous, even malevolent creatures. The hob is a generic term for a range of mischievous and malevolent spirits such as boggarts, bogles and brownies. Other variations include goblins, poltergeists, hobgoblins and bogeymen. The use of the term varies in different areas and countries. Bogle and boggart are native mainly to northern England, the Scottish Borders and Lincolnshire. The boggart is primarily devious and frightening; it never shows itself but plays tricks on people such as knocking books off shelves, slamming doors or tripping people up. It is also thought to punch, scratch and kick and is mainly active at night. In parts of Yorkshire the threat of being thrown into the 'boggart hole' was, and may still be, used by parents if their children misbehaved.

An old story of a hob comes from the *Whitby Magazine* of 1828 and concerns one that haunted a farmer and his wife on the North York Moors at Farndale in the mid-eighteenth century. The farmer, Jonathan Grey, had employed a young servant called Ralph to help out with the chores. However, tragedy struck the poor servant who was frozen to death in the snow after returning from an evening visit to the local fair. Some time after his death unusual noises were heard in the house and barn of the Grey family. Jonathan checked the barn to see where the noises were coming from, and to his amazement he saw that the corn had been threshed. Not knowing who was responsible for this welcome task they left the visitor a jug of cream with items of food.

This cycle of events – work being done and food and drink placed for the unknown worker – went on for some years. However, the cycle was broken when Jonathan's wife, Marjory, died and he remarried. His new wife cut back on the food and replaced the cream with skimmed milk. Such meanness clearly offended the unknown visitor, who stopped doing the work from that day forward. That might have not been so bad but the visitor resorted to a constant menacing of the couple. It is believed that when a brownie is teased or misused, it turns into a boggart and this seemed to be the case here. At first the poultry died, and then strange noises were heard at night and bedclothes were pulled off the bed. So desperate were the couple that they called in a local minister to undertake exorcisms, but these did not stop the problem. The only course of action left was to leave the farm and move elsewhere. As Jonathan was packing he heard a voice that asked what he was doing. Startled and frightened, Jonathan looked around and then replied 'flitting'. The malevolent little hob then responded in a terrifying voice, 'yes we're flitting.' Jonathan knew there was no escape from the evil spirit and resigned himself to staying at the farm and hoped that the hob would go away.

The story circulated and became so popular that, years later, Sir Alfred Lord Tennyson (1809-1892) referred to it in his poem *Walking to the Mail* (1842):

Vex'd with a morbid devil in his blood …
his house, for so they say,
Was haunted with a jolly ghost, that shook
The curtains, whined in lobbies, tapt at doors,
And rummaged like a rat: no servant stay'd:

Runswick Bay.

> The farmer vext packs up his beds and chairs,
> And all his household stuff; and with his boy
> Betwixt his knees, his wife upon the tilt,
> Sets out, and meets a friend who hails him, 'What!
> You're flitting!' 'Yes, we're flitting,' says the ghost
> (For they had pack'd the thing among the beds).
> 'Oh, well,' says he, 'you flitting with us too –
> Jack, turn the horses' heads and home again'.

There are other tales of the mischievous activity of hobs or boggarts around the Whitby area, such as those at the secluded village of Runswick Bay. One of the features there, and one which draws many enthusiasts, are the rugged cliffs perforated by caves or 'hob holes' which were reputedly occupied by hobs. The Runswick hob allegedly cured whooping cough, hence mothers took their ailing children there and called out:

> Hob – hole Hob!
> My bairn's getten't kink-cough:
> Tak't off! Tak't off!

Revd J.C. Atkinson wrote of various types of hobs and fairies in his books *A Handbook for Ancient Whitby* (1882) and *Forty Years in a Moorland Parish* (1907). One story was told to him by an old woman of a friendly hob of Hart Hall, in Glaisdale about 10 miles from Whitby. Like the Farndale hob, it would do the threshing at night when people were asleep. The curiosity to see the strange night visitor got the better of a young farmhand who, one night, crept out into the moonlight to have a look in the barn. There he saw a small 'brown man' covered 'wi' hair', and wearing only a ragged old coarse smock thrashing about with great vigour. When he told the other young farmhands they took pity on the hob and made him a new smock made out of sacking which they laid out in the barn for him. The hob, however, was not pleased with the garment and protested that he was being treated like a common labourer and never came back again.

There is a Hob Hill further north at Upleatham and at Marske-by-the-sea, where an old story tells of how a church that had been demolished was rebuilt by hobmen. In Mulgrave Woods, which surrounds the medieval Mulgrave Castle, was Hob's Cave, the home of an unfriendly hob. The woods are also reputed to be haunted by a bogle or fairy, who was once so enraged by a farmer who called out to her that she cut his horse in two with the blow of a rush.

Fairies were said to visit the isolated dales and the North York Moors. Percy Shaw Jeffrey recounts a tale from 1650 in the diary of Major Fairfax-Blakeborough. One early morning in May three men and a woman set off to walk to Whitby when they saw many fairies dancing in a small close. The group watched the fairies for a while until they suddenly disappeared. The major also acknowledged seeing the fairies 'by mysen as late as a week ago'.

Eighteen

REVENGE OF THE SILK SHAWL

A story told in a number of books about Whitby concerns a group of old and desperate Whitby fishermen who turned to piracy in the late eighteenth century because of several bad seasons of fishing. One of their pirating exploits involved the capture of an unlucky ship and even unluckier crew, who were ordered to walk the plank. Among the unfortunate captives were the captain of the ship and his wife who had been accompanying him on the journey. As the wife walked the plank to her death she was wearing a very beautiful silk shawl. This proved too much of a temptation to one of the pirates who snatched it from the shoulders of the woman and took it home as a gift for his wife. Predictably, he did not tell his wife how he had come by the shawl. As she placed it around her shoulders and looked admiringly at it in the mirror, suddenly to her horror, she saw a ghostly grey face behind her. It was the face of the drowned women who was pointing a bony hand accusingly at the shawl. The woman wearing the shawl went mad with terror and died shortly after. What happened to the shawl remains a mystery.

Fishing boats in the harbour.

Nineteen

THE HAUNTED HOUSE

Erected in 1900, the George Hotel (formerly the Station Hotel) was purpose built near the bus and railway stations. However, this ghost story does not relate to the George but to a fine old house which stood next door to the hotel. Dr John Ripley, who came to practice medicine in Whitby in 1812, once occupied the house. Years later, a strange sighting in the window of the house became a regular feature and began to draw crowds. Opposite the house stood some gardens and it was here that people started to congregate in anticipation of witnessing the movement of a ghost through the windows in the upper floor of the building. For groups of people to witness a ghost is unusual, as sightings tend to be witnessed by solitary individuals. However, for the occupants the combination of the hauntings and the continued attention of the gathering crowds became intolerable and they moved to Brunswick House. The vacated house developed such an evil reputation that no one wanted to live there and it was eventually pulled down.

Twenty

THE GHOST OF NUNNINGTON HALL

Nunnington Hall is approximately 20 miles south-west of Whitby. It is a mainly seventeenth-century manor house situated in Ryedale and a popular local attraction. The west wing dates from 1580 but was badly damaged during the Civil War by a Parliamentarian garrison. It was extensively rebuilt in 1685 and again in the 1920s. It is also noted for its haunted room and the attics, so much so that it has become the focus for Living TV's *Most Haunted* programme which searched for paranormal activity.

One particular story concerns that of the ghost of a wicked stepmother who apparently roams the manor house. The story has been passed down over generations but tells of a Lord of Nunnington, who was left with an only son to look after when his wife died. He eventually remarried an attractive young woman, who hated the stepson she had inherited. Shortly after the marriage the woman had a baby, a boy, and this meant she excluded her stepson even more. When her husband died, life for the stepson became unbearable as her cruelty towards him increased. Not surprisingly, she wanted all the inheritance to go to her own son. Staff felt sympathy for the stepson but did not dare to help him for fear of reprisals from the woman who kept a close eye on anything she deemed to be suspicious.

As she lived her life of luxury the poor boy was almost starved of food. Ironically, the one person who did comfort him and bring him food was his stepbrother, who he loved dearly. One day the cruelty became too much for the boy and he escaped from the hall. No one heard from him again and it was rumoured he had run away to sea and had possibly drowned. His departure pleased the horrid stepmother, but the young brother was heartbroken and could never accept he had left. He continued to search the hall shouting his name and it was the searching that caused his own death. By leaning out of a window looking for his brother he fell onto the gravel walk below and died. The woman was devastated and sat for hours lamenting her loss. On other occasions she would wander to the painted room constantly looking for him. When she eventually died and other people occupied the house they heard the sounds of footsteps and the rustling of a silk dress dashing up the staircase. She has also been seen to open the door of the leather room, and look out of the window.

Over the years, staff have reported hearing strange things in parts of the hall including the panelled room, and seeing the figure of a woman in the garden.

Twenty-one

THE GHOST OF KITTY

This tale concerns a young single girl called Kitty, who lived in Farndale and was in love with a rich young farmer. However, there was a problem – Kitty became pregnant by the farmer. So distraught was the young girl she begged to meet the father. On a stormy night the girl waited near the local pub but the man did not show. Her fears were confirmed when a man who was passing spotted her and told her that he had seen someone resembling the young farmer riding off in the opposite direction. Devastated by the news the girl threw herself into the river which had swollen by the heavy rain. To add to the tragedy the young man was also found dead with a wedding ring in his pocket. Clearly he was on his way to meet Kitty that night and had not been the man riding off on a horse.

Because poor Kitty had committed suicide, she had to suffer the burial reserved for those who committed this offence, until 1823 when the law was repealed: she was buried at a crossroads with a stake driven through her. The restless ghost of Kitty haunted the area around the river where she had died, but each anniversary she came to claim a victim. So troubled were local people that one couple resolved that the only way to exorcise Kitty's ghost was to dig up her remains and rebury her in an appropriate burial ground. Her ghost never appeared again.

Twenty-two

THE GOLDSBOROUGH GHOST

In his book, *Ghosts and Yorkshire's Legends* (1983), Terence Whitaker relates how in 1904, Edward Daniel Walker, a former mayor of Darlington (1901-2) and owner of the *Northern Echo*, told of an incident when he was a child. He lived with his family in the village of Goldsborough, 5 miles north of Whitby, because his father was a coastguard and had been posted to the village in the 1860s. When they first arrived at Goldsborough on a cart with all their belongings, there was no accommodation for them, so they stayed at a local inn for a few days. Eventually they were able to rent the wing of a farmhouse which had been unoccupied for a number of years.

Within less than a month of living in the farmhouse the father came home one night at around midnight. He set about making himself supper when suddenly the fender from the fireplace started to lift up from the hearth. It did this three times before falling with a loud bang. He also heard the noise of the closet door opening and closing. The noises woke his wife who came downstairs to see what was happening. She saw her husband sitting in the kitchen looking puzzled as to what could be making the sounds and causing such a rumpus.

A month later the wife was asleep in bed with their baby when the movement of the bed awakened her. Struck with fear she clung to the child as the bed was raised from the ground three times. The woman screamed and stayed in the bed, terrified of moving from it. An hour later her husband returned and as she was recounting what had happened they both heard a noise from outside that sounded like two dogs fighting. When the man dashed outside to see what was causing the commotion he found nothing.

The strange happenings prompted the coastguard to find out more about the house and its previous occupants. He asked the old widow who lived in the adjoining part of the farmhouse. Apart from being told that some previous tenants had moved out after only staying for a short time, his initial enquiries proved rather fruitless. A few days later a joiner was called in to fix a window in the boy's bedroom. As the joiner worked on the window he almost froze with fear as he saw the figure of a man draped in white appear from nowhere and proceed to walk across the room and then vanish as quickly as he had appeared. The joiner abandoned his tools and fled the house in terror.

The old widow who shared the house died a year after this incident and the man bought the rest of the property. He then started the task of renovating it by removing some of the areas that had given rise to the strange occurrences, such as the flagstones in the kitchen and in particular the old hearthstone. As he dug out the hearth he came across a rather macabre discovery, which explained the mysterious activity: a human skeleton. The family never found out who the skeleton was or how long it had been there but the hauntings did cease.

Twenty-three

THE DEVIL

The most evil manifestation of a supernatural form is the Devil, who goes by various names and features in many religions. The Devil is believed to be a powerful evil entity that is usually portrayed as fighting over the souls of humans and commands a force of lesser evil spirits known as demons. As with poltergeist activity, demons are said to manipulate physical objects as well as people. They are even present in the Bible where they are responsible for causing fires, possessing people, creating great winds and inflicting ailments. Many believe hauntings can be explained by one of a number of reasons: the visiting or summoning of the dead (via spirit guides, or helpers such as mediums, Ouija boards or séances); the chicanery of charlatans; and demonic activity. The Devil, it would appear, has haunted Whitby and its surrounding area, and this is apparent in a number of stories. For example:

- Smoke produced from rubbing jet was believed to drive away the devil and his demons.
- The tale told earlier of the card-playing smugglers who sat with the 'Gentleman in Black'.
- The barguest or large black dog is believed to be the devil in disguise. Dracula appeared as a dog, thus justifying claims that the devil appears in different forms.
- Bells (notably the old abbey bells) have, according to tradition, the power to drive away the devil and all his agents.
- The Hand of Glory were sometimes used in ceremonies to the Devil.
- Hobs have been linked with the Devil.
- The Hole of Horcum is also referred to as 'the Devil's punchbowl'.
- The legend of St Hilda, who drove an infestation of snakes, which are representational of the Devil.
- Witches were often accused of making satanic pacts.

Older superstitions involved precautions against evil and the Devil.

In the 1660s an old 'enchantress', Molly Milburn of Danby, specialized in amulets of 'skinne' with silken thread to keep evil spirits away but was eventually whipped for being a witch. In 1780 Ann Allan of Ugthorpe was feared for her knowledge of the 'Black Art' as well as possessing the power of the evil eye. She was accused of letting the devil affect the milking of cows in her village. In the eighteenth century Nan Hardwick of Danby Dale was also believed to have the evil eye which could turn people into statues. Meg Collett-Richardson from Sleights was ducked and drowned in 1719 for practicing evil spells. However, these are examples of poor, unfortunate women who became the victims of those with superstitious fears rather than the agents of the Devil.

Twenty-four

GHOST WALK ITINERARY

This itinerary shows locations mentioned in the book as well as additional stories and information in relation to specific places in the town. It can be used for reference or, better still, for you to walk. It is feasible to do the walk in one go but you may not feel compelled to do this, or indeed to take precisely the route marked out. If you make further discoveries and get sidetracked, so much the better. Whitby also offers well-organised and entertaining ghost walks.

1. Royal Crescent

The building of Royal Crescent in the 1850s was the inspiration of the 'Railway King' and entrepreneur, George Hudson (1800-1871). His railway link to Whitby opened up the town to tourism and a new source of income. The building of guest houses and hotels were developed on the West Cliff. The Royal Crescent is only half-built because Hudson ran out of money. The Royal Hotel was a favourite haunt of Bram Stoker. The top floor of the hotel was reputedly host to strange noises and activity. Apparently, when a wall was knocked down in the building, an alcove was found with the remains of a body.

There is a Bram Stoker memorial seat installed in April 1980 opposite the Royal Hotel. The location of the seat depicts a view in *Dracula* where Mina Murray looked out one night and recorded the view of the harbour and the churchyard.

Since at least 1905, people have reported a haunting 'mysterious white wraith', a transparent apparition along the area of West Cliff beach.

Near the Royal Crescent is the Whalebone Arch, which was presented to Whitby by Norway in 1963. It stands as a reminder of the old whaling industry in which many Whitby men were killed over the years as a result of boats being overturned and ships crushed.

2. Number Seven Guest House, No. 7 East Crescent

The house was built in 1847 and is referred to in various publications as the house that was occupied by Count Dracula's lawyer, Samuel F. Billington – No. 7, The Crescent, Whitby (Chapter 3, 'Jonathan Harker's Journal'). Colin Waters, author of *Whitby: Then & Now*, *Bygone Whitby*, and *Whitby: A Pictorial History*, suggests that the name Harker was borrowed from Fanny Harker, Stoker's landlady in Whitby. Note also the nearby passage (see 'Creepy Tunnel' earlier).

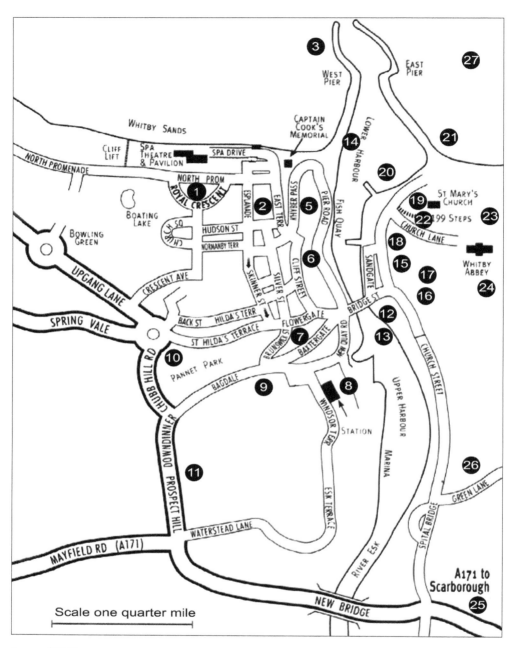

A map of Whitby town centre.

Royal Crescent.

The Whalebone Arch.

No. 7 East Crescent.

3. Lighthouse and West Pier

Whitby has two piers and two lighthouses in its harbour. The west lighthouse, built in 1835 (the older and taller, at 83ft) is worked manually and is used only when vessels are expecting an indication that it is safe to enter the harbour. The east lighthouse, built in 1855, is 54ft high.

In the 1950s, in the west pier lighthouse, there was an account of a girl who was climbing the stairs with her mother when she saw the ghost of a man.

4. Harbourside

The custom of the planting of the Penny Hedge (or Horngarth, as it is sometimes called) takes place every year on the eve of Ascension Day. The Penny Hedge ceremony is believed to date back to 1159 when a hermit monk from Whitby Abbey hid a wild boar from three noblemen and refused to let them kill it. The wounded boar took refuge in the chapel and hermitage at Eskdaleside, which was occupied by the hermit. Enraged, the hunters beat the hermit so badly he eventually died, but not before he managed to tell the abbot of what had happened. He pleaded with the abbot that the men should not be prosecuted for their foul deed, on condition that they and their successors paid a penance for their sins. What was the penance? On the sunrise of every Ascension Day, these men or their successors should collect staves from Eskdaleside and the price should not exceed more than one penny. The staves should then be carried to Whitby before nine o' clock on that morning and then planted in the mud in the harbour. A small hedge would then be weaved strong enough to withstand three tides. If the hedge failed the three tides, then all the lands of the men or their successors would be forfeited to the abbot of Whitby or his successors. For 800 years the hedge survived the three tides, but in 1981 the site was covered by 8ft of sea water. The successors were

A view through the tunnel near the arch, towards Whitby Abbey.

Lighthouse, west pier.

View looking towards Whitby with the harbour in the far distance. Between the mid-eighteenth to the mid-nineteenth centuries, the area from the bridge to what is now the marina car park was a busy area of shipyards, roperies and sail yards.

subsequently released from the penance. Nonetheless, the custom continues each year and the ceremony prescribed by the monk is carried out by the occupiers of the land formerly owned by the abbot. The horn is sounded by the bailiff to the lady of the manor, and followed by the cry 'Out on ye, Out on ye.'

5. Dracula Experience, No. 9 Marine Parade

The 'Dracula Experience' is a tourist attraction where visitors can wander through the darkness and hear sinister music while animated characters re-enact the story. A cape worn by Christopher Lee in his second *Dracula* film is on show.

There are also themed Dracula walks in the town. You might want to walk parts of Whitby mentioned in Stoker's book (see also the section on *Dracula*).

6. Haggersgate

With an unusual name, Hagg or Hag appears often in names around the moors and towns: Hagg House, Hagg Farm, Hags Wood, and Haggersgate and Haggerlythe at Whitby. The meaning of the word varies from place to place and, in times gone by, hag referred to woodland, especially on a sloping bank. Another meaning of hag is an ugly, old woman or a witch. Around the moors are hag-stones, pieces of flint with a natural hole in them, which country people of former times thought were lucky charms to keep witches away. However, hag can also refer to boggy areas, patches of marshland or an area of higher or drier land which is raised above the surrounding bog. Gate is the old Nordic word for street or path.

There have been stories of a phantom coach heard driving near the ancient street of Haggersgate before stopping outside the Whitby Mission. After a few minutes it then drives away. In 1793, Whitby sailors rose against the hated pressgang in Haggersgate. One old man, for his part in this serious riot, was hanged at York.

7. Old Smuggler (Baxtergate)

The building, which is now the Old Smuggler café, was referred to by George Young in his *History of Whitby and Streoneshalh Abbey* (1817). He commented that an 'excellent house at Baxtergate stood long empty as it had obtained the character of being visited by ghosts: it is now frequented by spirits of another kind

The 'Dracula Experience'.

having been converted into an inn'. It was popularly thought that the old building had an underground passage that led to the quayside, which in earlier times served as a tunnel for smugglers.

8. Railway Station

A railway station in Whitby features in *Dracula*. Mina Murray records how 'Lucy met me at the station, looking sweeter and lovelier than ever, and we drove up to the house at the Crescent …' The present station, which was opened in 1846 by the York & North Midland Railway, was built to the design of its architect, George Townsend Andrews. They 'drove up to the house', which suggests this might have been the station where they met. However, there was another station in Whitby on the West Cliff near the Crescent. This was built to develop the West Cliff area but it fell victim to the railway cuts in the 1960s.

9. Bagdale Hall

Bagdale Hall is haunted by a number of ghosts, including the headless spirit of one its previous owners, Browne Bushell (1609-1651). Note the stone carvings of heads outside the hall.

The Old Smuggler.

The railway station.

10. Whitby Museum

Walk past Bagdale Hall and onto Chub Hill. This will bring you to Pannett Park and the Whitby Museum, which is part of the Whitby Literary & Philosophical Society. The park is named after Alderman Robert Elliott Pannett (1834-1920), who bequeathed land in 1920 to develop a public park, museum and art gallery. The macabre and sinister 'Hand of Glory' is one of the exhibits.

The museum might be visited separately and the walk could continue from Bagdale Hall over the Swing Bridge picking up on Grape Lane (12) – the first turn right over the bridge.

11. Prospect Hill

The area between Prospect Hill and Ruswarp is reputedly haunted by a headless male entity, who walks around the area carrying his head grasped under his arm.

12. Grape Lane

The name has little to do with vines or grapes. Grape Lane, which is part of Whitby's Old Town, is a corruption of Grope Lane. Before street lighting was introduced, people used to 'grope their way down this dark street.' It might also have something to do with other forms of groping!

A cottage hospital was moved here in 1901. As a result of an unfortunate accident a young girl was brought to the hospital after being burned in a bakery in 1917, but died from her injuries. Her ghost was said to haunt the building even when it was no longer used for medical care.

Bagdale Hall.

Stone carving outside Bagdale Hall.

Stone carving outside Bagdale Hall.

Whitby Museum.

13. Captain Cook Memorial Museum, Grape Lane

Before Captain James Cook set out on his famous voyages, he was apprenticed in 1746 for three years to the Quaker ship-owner, Captain John Walker of Grape Lane. The seventeenth-century grade 1 listed house is now preserved as the Captain Cook Memorial Museum. Not surprisingly such an old house has its share of ghost stories. Among those who haunt the house is a housekeeper called Mary who worked there, and also a young girl aged between eight and ten years of age, whose father was a sailor.

14. Endeavour Public House, Church Street

Named after Cook's famous ship, this pub is featured as one of the haunted stories in *13 Ghost Stories from Whitby* (1999) by Michael Wray, and concerns the ghost of a young blonde-haired girl.

Grape Lane.

15. Shambles Market Square

Whitby's Market Square can be traced back to 1640. The Town Hall in the square was built by local notable Nathaniel Cholmley much later, in 1788. The Shambles Bar & Restaurant is believed to be haunted by a man who died in a fire in a building on that site prior to the Shambles being built.

16. White Horse and Griffin, Church Street

This hotel first opened its doors in 1681, and in 1788 the first stagecoach left Whitby for the 50-mile journey to York from the inn. Many distinguished figures have passed through the place including George Stephenson and Charles Dickens. The building has associations with various hauntings.

The Captain Cook Museum.

The Endeavour pub.

The Shambles.

17. The Black Horse Inn

There has been a drinking establishment on the site of the Black Horse Inn for many centuries. In fact, it was previously called the White Horse Inn until it changed the name in 1828. As one of the oldest pubs in Whitby, it has had a number of ghost stories associated with it. Established in 1600, it later became a funeral directors, spirit warehouse and brothel. Like its nearby neighbour, the White Horse and Griffin, the Black Horse has been frequented by many illustrious people and it is believed that Bram Stoker, Elizabeth Gaskell, Lewis Carroll and Wilkie Collins visited there. The pub was also notorious for its involvement with smuggling and there are stories of secret passages, false panels and trap doors (long since sealed) which provided both escape routes and places to hide contraband.

18. Church Street

Church Street is one of the oldest streets in Whitby. It was said that smuggled goods could travel from one end of Church Street to another, without ever touching the ground. Sightings of a phantom wearing a black cloak have been seen crossing Church Street from the Market Square and walking past the Black Horse Inn. It is believed to be that of an old 'knocker-upper' who used to wake railway workers early in the morning.

19. Whitby Jet Heritage Centre

Whitby's involvement with jet goes back many centuries. However, the first jet workshop was not established until 1808. At its peak there were over 200 jet workshops in Whitby, but the industry was in decline by the 1890s. There is a handful of skilled local craftsman producing jewellery from Whitby Jet. Note the Whitby Jet Heritage Centre located at the end of Church Street.

The White Horse and Griffin.

The Black Horse Inn.

Church Street – the main street through the old town. Whitby has many yards, steps and houses which reflect a distinctively nautical atmosphere.

Old Town Hall and Market Square. Look out for the mysterious 'knocker-upper' who walks across here dressed in black.

Kipper Shop.

Jet is thought to have mystical powers and as such it serves as a potent talisman and protective agent. In his small and informative booklet, *The Story of Whitby Jet* (1936), the former Honorary Curator of Whitby Museum, Hugh P. Kendall, commented that jet crosses were used as charms against witchcraft.

20. Henrietta Street

Where the 199 steps meet Church Street is Henrietta Street, previously called Haggerlyth. Henrietta Street was named after the second wife of local notable Nathaniel Cholmley. It is along here that a phantom funeral coach, drawn by six black horses with two outriders wearing black and bearing blazing torches, thunders along at great speed before it eventually plunges over the cliff at the end of the road and into the sea. If you walk down this road during the day you will see a Whitby institution: Fortune's Kippers, which was established in 1872. Racks of kippers can be seen hanging above smouldering oak wood chips in the smokehouse. To my knowledge, it is not haunted!

21. East Cliff

At the junction of the 199 steps and Henrietta Street, Tate Hill Pier can be seen. Another view would be from the far end of Henrietta Street as it runs into the cliffside. The significance of this stretch of beach is made clear in *Dracula*, as the *Demeter* crashes onto the sands with its terrifying cargo:

> A great awe came on all as they realised that the ship, as if by a miracle, had found the harbour, unsteered save by the hand of a dead man … The schooner paused not, but rushing across the harbour, pitched herself on that accumulation of sand and gravel washed by many tides and many storms into the southeast corner of the pier jutting under the East Cliff, known locally as Tate Hill Pier. There was of course a considerable

Henrietta Street.

concussion as the vessel drove up on the sand heap … It so happened that there was no one at the moment on Tate Hill Pier, as all those whose houses are in close proximity were either in bed or were out on the heights above.

22. The 199 Steps

First mentioned over 600 years ago, the 199 steps link Church Street with St Mary' Church and the abbey. As Mina Murray noted in her journal in *Dracula*, 'The steps are a great feature on the place. They lead from the town to the church … I do not know how many, and they wind up in a delicate curve.'

For those who feel the need to rest or stop and admire the view, there are regular resting places. No doubt the pallbearers would have appreciated these on funeral days. Running parallel to the steps is the cobble-stoned Church Lane or 'Donkey Road' which was used for processions on feast days.

23. St Mary's Church and Graveyard

The church was built between 1110 and 1120, and in fact predates the ruins of the Abbey by 100 years. In *Dracula*, Mina Murray makes a number of references to St Mary's Church and the graveyard (see the section on *Dracula* earlier). It plays an important role in the first sighting of the vampire: 'What it was, whether man or beast, I could not tell'.

The evil that lurked in the graveyard contrasts sharply with a more serene comment on the churchyard where 'people go and sit there all day long looking at the beautiful view and enjoying the breeze'.

The graveyard is also associated with the story of how a headless ghost driving a coach-like funeral hearse would appear beside the grave of a deceased sailor at night, ready to take him away. There have also been sightings of a headless figure clad in white.

199 Steps from the bottom.

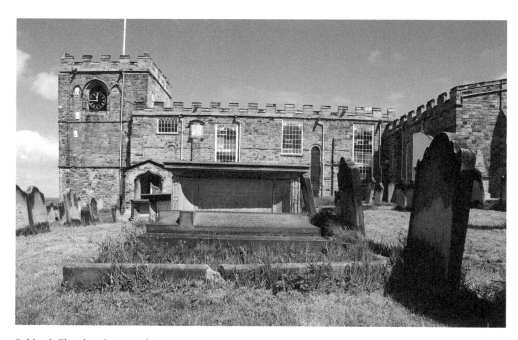

St Mary's Church and graveyard.

Caedmon Cross is a memorial to the first English poet whose vision is described in the section on the abbey. The Cross is made in imitation Saxon style and was unveiled in September 1898 by Poet Laureate Alfred Austin.

24. The Abbey

Founded in AD 657, the abbey was destroyed by the Danes in the ninth century. The present ruins date from when the abbey was rebuilt from 1220. However, the abbey suffered destruction in 1540 during the reign of Henry VIII. The following hauntings and stories are associated with the abbey:

- Sightings of the ghost of St Hilda. Crowds from far and wide would gather at the west side of the churchyard, between 10 and 11 in the morning. When the sun shone on the window it created an illusion of a woman's form wrapped in a shroud. This optical illusion was presumed to be that of Hilda and tradition grew that she also walked the abbey as a phantom.
- The sounds of choirs singing early in the morning when no one else was present.
- Ammonites are said to be the petrified remains of snakes that once plagued the Whitby area, until Hilda decapitated them with her whip and drove them over the edge of the cliff where they then turned into stone.
- The headless body of King Edwin (586-633) was a notable burial at Whitby Abbey.
- St Cuthbert of Lindisfarne (635-687) saw the ghostly apparition of a shepherd named Hadwald.
- The myth of the ghost of Constance de Beverley, a young Whitby nun, is said to haunt the abbey ruins.
- The bells of Whitby Abbey, when taken during the Reformation, sank the ship carrying them to London. The bells have been heard ringing out from the sea that took them.
- In recent years, the *Whitby Gazette* reported a panther-like creature stalking the area around the abbey.

Whitby Abbey.

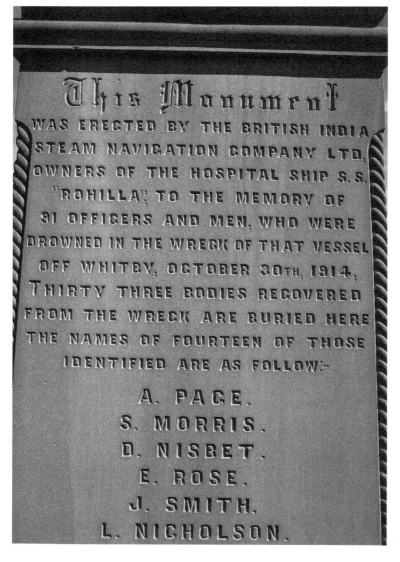

This Monument

WAS ERECTED BY THE BRITISH INDIA
STEAM NAVIGATION COMPANY LTD,
OWNERS OF THE HOSPITAL SHIP S.S.
"ROHILLA", TO THE MEMORY OF
91 OFFICERS AND MEN, WHO WERE
DROWNED IN THE WRECK OF THAT VESSEL
OFF WHITBY, OCTOBER 30TH, 1914,
THIRTY THREE BODIES RECOVERED
FROM THE WRECK ARE BURIED HERE
THE NAMES OF FOURTEEN OF THOSE
IDENTIFIED ARE AS FOLLOW:-

A. PAGE.
S. MORRIS.
D. NISBET.
E. ROSE.
J. SMITH.
L. NICHOLSON.

The *Rohilla* memorial.

- The Whitby Wyrm. The legend tells of a dragon-like serpent that was disturbed from his slumber during the building of the abbey. He attempted to destroy the town but was banished into the sea. Every seven years he supposedly returns at full moon to attempt to drag the abbey into the sea by clawing away at the cliff on which it stands.

25. Whitby Cemetery

The *Rohilla* memorial commemorates those who lost their lives in the shipwreck of October 1914. Those who were recovered were interred in Whitby Cemetery whilst others were claimed by relatives and buried in their home towns. The British India Steam Navigation Co. Ltd, *Rohilla*'s company, erected the memorial.

The cemetery reflects the association of the town with fishing as carvings of anchors and boats mark many graves.

Caption on the *Rohilla* memorial.

26. Greenlane Area

For anyone feeling fit enough to do the coastal walk from Whitby to Robin Hood's Bay, there will be a good deal of beautiful scenery to take in and you might keep an eye out for the mysterious fisherman as you approach the lighthouse. Mina Murray and Lucy took the walk in *Dracula* where they enjoyed tea at Robin Hood's Bay.

Along this stretch the ghostly sounds of the shipwreck victims have been heard from Robin Hood's Bay, such as those from the *Rohilla*.

27. Lighthouse

Built in 1858, altered in 1890 and automated in 1992 when a more efficient light was installed, the Trinity House Lighthouse is over a mile south of the town. Look out for the ghostly 'fisherman', first seen in the late 1980s, who carries a basket of fish and disappears when walking towards the lighthouse.

Twenty-five

A-Z OF HAUNTED SITES AROUND WHITBY

Aislaby Hall

Aislaby Hall is a curious and interesting old house, built in the eighteenth century. Guests and inhabitants have heard the rustling of a lady moving around in a silken dress, going down the main staircase – hence she was christened with the nickname 'Rustling'. This figure has never been seen but the sounds of her moving have been quite distinctive. This is in contrast to the sighting of a large phantom coach being driven outside the hall.

Burniston

The Three Jolly Sailors in Burniston, to the north of Scarborough, is a seventeenth-century pub haunted by an old parson and an old sailor. The sailor apparently sits on a wooden log in front of the fire and, needless to say, it is unlucky for anyone who removes the log. This legend of the sailor's spirit dates back to the pub's alleged connection with smuggling. The ghost of the parson originates from many years ago when part of the building used to be chapel. The ghost is believed to still visit the pub daily between 10 and 11 a.m., appearing in the restaurant.

Cloughton

The village before Burniston is Cloughton where the Falcon Inn can be found. The former coaching inn, which marked the change-over point for horses making the journey between Scarborough and Whitby, has almost 200 years of history. It is haunted by the ghost of a lady that sits in the corner of the pub. She has been seen on many occasions and regulars have spoken of the toilet door which is supposed to open on its own, and the kettle in the kitchen is often on and boiling when it is unplugged.

Egton

The sighting of a large, ferocious black dog was recorded at Egton, about 7 miles from Whitby. The hound confronted a man near St Hilda's Church and began to chase him.

Farndale

Farndale lies some miles to the west of Whitby and is a remote little corner surrounded by moorland. There are at least two rather macabre stories associated with place. One concerns the hob that flitted with the family as outlined earlier in the book, and the other is regarding the ghost of Kitty.

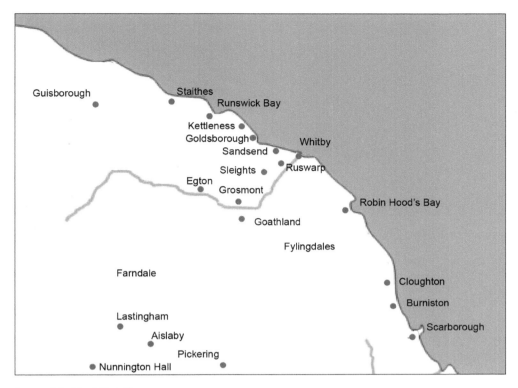

A map of the North York Moors.

Fylingdales

There have been many reports of unusual phenomena around the moors. In addition to unidentified flying objects there have been sightings of a cat-like creature. One witness reported seeing a large 'puma-like animal' that had evidently been hit by a car. As the man came nearer to the incident there was a police car and a tractor. The animal was being loaded into the police car. The man tried to get a better look by slowing down and the police officer told him to keep his mouth shut as they did not want to alarm the public. The man made further enquires, only to be met by a wall of silence with various authorities denying any knowledge of the incident.

Gisborough Hall

Gisborough Hall, a mansion built for Admiral Thomas Chaloner in 1856 just outside the town of Guisborough, is now a luxurious, country-house hotel run by Macdonald Hotels. It is reputed to have three resident ghosts haunting its stairways and bedrooms. A phantom butler walks the performing tasks that are no longer required. Another ghost haunts the lobby area (though can only be glimpsed out of the corner of one's eye), while a shadowy old woman haunts the old nursery.

Hole of Horcum, North York Moors.

RAF Fylingdales, North York Moors.

Gisborough Priory

The dramatic ruins of Gisborough Priory (founded in 1195), with its remaining 97ft-high gothic eastern gable towers, looks over the market town of Gisborough. On the first new moon of the year a monk, known as the Black Monk, makes an appearance to ensure that reputed buried treasure has not been discovered.

Goathland

Goathland is a village situated on the North York Moors off the A169 road near Whitby. It is surrounded by beautiful scenery and is famous for being the setting for the popular ITV police series *Heartbeat*.

Interesting connections with the supernatural at Goathland include:

- The Gytrash – a fearsome spectral dog which, according to legend, is the ghost of Julian de Maubrey. There is also the wailing of Gytha, the young maid he entombed within the walls of his castle.
- The story of the two witches who could take the form of cats and then cause mischief on the locals.
- The bogle house at Greenend.
- The ghosts of a tailor and a dead warrior.

Goldsborough

Goldsborough is approximately 5 miles north of Whitby. During the 1860s a farmhouse was haunted by strange noises, the slamming of doors and a bed being raised off the ground. When the house was later renovated a human skeleton was found under the flagstones in the kitchen.

Kettleness

Kettleness lies on the coast between Whitby and Staithes. Like a number of other places it also has bogles. These particular creatures lived at Claymore Well, a mile east of Kettleness.

Lastingham

Although a village that goes slightly beyond our parameters, Lastingham might be worth looking at for anyone travelling to Whitby from the west. It is a picturesque and fascinating village. Its fine church and long Christian tradition has attracted both tourists and pilgrims. The most interesting feature of the church is the crypt which was built in 1078 as a shrine to St Cedd, a Lindisfarne monk who founded the first monastery here in AD 654. The crypt was designed as a miniature church, with apse, nave and side aisles. Once in the crypt, it is claimed that paranormal vibes are distinctly felt. Many have testified to its power. The editor of the *Northern Earth* magazine (P. Heselton, 'The Power of Lastingham Crypt', *Northern Earth Mysteries* 5, 1980) commented that a friend of his who spent some time down there felt unable to speak afterwards. Others have said that they felt some 'supernatural presence' in the crypt. The church is believed to be haunted. Mike Haigh, writing in *Northern Earth* (67), stated that the canon said he often experienced a 'discarnate spirit' in the church. Haigh added that two people noted 'that a compass they placed in the crypt continued moving with a rhythmic jigging'.

Mulgrave Woods

Situated north-west of Whitby, the woods are reputed to be haunted by a bogle or fairy.

North York Moors

The approach to Whitby from Pickering offers one of the finest landscapes in Britain. The North York Moors National Park covers miles of moorland, heather, beaches and grassy dales. Also along the A169 is RAF Fylingdales, easily identified by the concrete 'pyramid' seen from the road. Fylingdales is a long-range radar station, which forms part of the Ballistic Missile Early Warning System and Space Surveillance Network. It also keeps track of spy satellites used by other countries.

Unsurprisingly, such a vast and atmospheric setting has produced many reports of eerie phenomena. One of the strange hauntings in the area is of UFOs. The *Yorkshire Post* (11 August 2005) reported that there had been over eighty-five sightings around North Yorkshire, and that the area between Whitby, the moors and as far south as Filey is considered to be the UFO-spotting capital of Britain. The *Whitby Gazette* (2 March 2007) wrote that an eighteen-year-old local man said he saw an unusual object hovering silently in the vicinity of Staithes. He described it as having about eight red and orange lights. On 30 October 2007 the *Whitby Gazette* ran the news that 'Mysterious lights were spotted over Whitby Abbey last week – prompting reports of a possible UFO sighting'.

Another witness reported that he and his wife were travelling late one evening across the Whitby Moors. As they stopped to look at the night sky they spotted what appeared to be a large star. There were other objects moving up and down next to the white object which then moved off at great speed. Terrified, they ran to their car and sped off towards Whitby.

The terrifying Barguest creature, or at least an abnormally large black dog, has also been seen on many occasions on the moors.

Nunnington Hall

Although some 20 miles south-west of Whitby, the seventeenth-century manor house situated here is of particular interest, notably for the ghost story of the awful stepmother and the poor stepson. Ghostly activities include the sounds of footsteps, the rustling of a silk dress dashing up the staircase and the ghost of a woman looking out of a window and walking in the garden.

Pickering Castle

The ghost of a tall, gliding monk clad in grey clothing with a hood pulled over his head was seen in 1951 and 1970. The robed figure drifted across the lawn outside the front of the castle and then disappeared. One witness described it as having what looked like a bloody face and carrying an unknown object.

Robin Hood's Bay

The origin of the name remains something of a mystery. There is no evidence that Robin Hood visited the bay although there are a number of accounts as to where the name originated from. It is more likely that the name grew from legends with local origin.

The bay gained a reputation for being the busiest smuggling community on the Yorkshire coast and, whilst there are ghost stories, many of them are associated with smuggling and were probably largely invented as a means of keeping people indoors whilst the illegal activities went on.

Although smuggling and piracy presented its problems for local law enforcement, there were other issues that needed to be dealt with. By the late nineteenth century the coastal area around Robin Hood's Bay witnessed an influx of navvy labour working on the coastal railway between Whitby and Scarborough. Saturday was payday and the beer flowed among the men. Lubricated with plenty of ale, entertainment was sought which often meant fighting the locals on the beach, usually resulting in various broken heads, arms, legs and other parts of the body. On one occasion someone was killed. It was felt that a prison and police station was needed and so one was built in 1886 at a cost of £1,500 – although prisoners were very few. As the years passed there was less of a need for the station and it was subsequently sold in 1941 to a family who named the building Beckfield.

Runswick Bay

A few miles further north is Runswick Bay, a secluded picturesque village. In 1682, as villagers attended a wake, the original village of Runswick Bay slid into the sea as a result of a landslip. The only house that did not was that of the dead man.

Caves, or 'hob holes', are reputedly occupied by hobs.

Robin Hood's Bay.

Beckfield.

Ruswarp

'Goosey's ghost' haunts the road between Ruswarp and Sleights, 2-3 miles west of Whitby. Goosey was the nickname given to a man who bet he could eat a whole goose in one sitting. He failed on his first attempt but succeeded on the second. It was some time after this event that Goosey's body was found in the river. It was believed he had been murdered (nothing to do with either the goose or the wager!) although there was no proof. Goosey's ghost came back to haunt the banks of the Esk for many years as well as the village, particularly whenever an accident seemed imminent.

Saltersgate Inn, Saltersgate

The Saltergate Inn, built in 1760, is on the moors between Pickering and Whitby, close to RAF Fylingdales. According to a well-known story, if the fire at the Saltergate Inn ever went out, the ghost of a Customs and Excise officer would haunt the village. It is believed that the spirit of the man, whose body was buried under the fire by smugglers, will bring plague. A variation on this story suggests that the fire had to be kept burning in order to keep the malignant evil spirit of a witch buried by the burning of peat. Will the bluff now be called, as the pub closed down and was seeking planning permission in February 2008 to convert it into thirteen holiday homes?

Another haunting is the sound of a woman crying, not inside the inn but floating from across the moors. Could these be the cries of Gytha, the young maid?

The nearby Hole of Horcum, 'the Devil's punchbowl', is a vast, crater-like stretch of moor 120m deep and more than 1km across, scooped out by thousands of years of spring-water erosion. Legend has it that the Devil, in removing earth and boulders, left the depression in the ground.

Sandsend

Sandsend is 2½ miles north of Whitby. Keep an eye out for a large mysterious creature reported in the *Whitby Gazette* in 2006. The animal was described as 'enormous' – 4ft high and 3ft wide.

Look out for the old disused Sandsend Rail Tunnel where sightings include white lights, figures passing through walls and the sound of a steam train.

Scarborough

Scarborough, which is 20 miles south of Whitby, is generally recognized as Britain's first seaside resort with a history of welcoming visitors for over 360 years. The town was founded well over 1,000 years ago as Skarthaborg. It was an important centre for tradesmen from all over England as well as people from overseas, and this was reflected in the song *Scarborough Fair*. It was not a fair in the traditional sense but a huge forty-five day trading event, starting in August of each year from the thirteenth to the eighteenth century. As the importance of the harbour declined, so did the fair.

The town has a number of ghostly associations:

- The Pink Lady, Lydia Bell, was strangled to death on Scarborough beach. The Georgian house in St Nicholas Street, where Lydia stayed with her family, was built in 1708 for her father who was a York confectioner. The family visited Scarborough every year, but it was in 1804 when teenager Lydia became attracted to a young officer who was stationed at Castle Hill Barracks. Lydia's father did not approve of the relationship and locked her in her room while he and Mrs Bell went out for the evening. Lydia, determined to meet the man, managed to free herself from her room with the help of a neighbour. Dressed in a pink frock she looked forward to her date. Tragically, she was found murdered on the beach the following morning. The officer was charged but he was acquitted for lack

Sandsend with Runswick Bay in the distance. Look out for the Barghest creature which has been sighted in Sandsend.

Scarborough Harbour.

of evidence. Many years later another man confessed to the murder on his deathbed. The ghost of Lydia returned to haunt the street and the house in St Nicholas Street, and a number of people have reported seeing the spectre. A couple who lived in the house sixty years ago said their young daughter cried because 'the lady in a frock would not let her into the garden', but there was no lady there when the couple went to look. After the Second World War the house was turned into flats and some people who stayed there experienced Lydia's ghost. An artist who painted the house included a lady in a pink dress going up the steps.

- A headless woman who warns fishermen of impending disasters reputedly haunts the old Three Mariners pub. A headless phantom would appear as a warning to any sailors staying in the building not to go to sea – those who did see her but ignored the warnings normally drowned.

- The Lancaster Inn on the foreshore is said to be the scene of a macabre double child murder and suicide.
- St Mary's Church is a famous church with an interesting history. In a detached part of the churchyard is buried Anne Bronte, who died on 28 May 1849, aged twenty-eight. Every year on 24 April – St Mark's Eve - it was the custom at many churches throughout the country for people to congregate around the graveyard and the church door. The apparition of all those who were to die between this date and next year's St Mark's Eve would appear on the stroke of midnight and walk into the church.
- Scalby Manor, built in 1885, was eventually turned into a guesthouse in the twentieth century until it became derelict in the 1990s. Whitbread's, the brewing company, bought it in 1995. A number of sightings of different ghosts have been recorded in the local papers over the years. For example, a woman in a white gown has been sitting at a dressing table combing her hair. Another was of two children, a little boy who stands in the entrance and a blonde-haired girl with red shoes. Also in the cellar – there is always something creepy about cellars – the ghostly figure of a man has been seen. The *Scarborough Evening News* reported two strange happenings that happened recently. In July 2005 restaurant staff said they were afraid to go alone into the cellars. One account told of the ghostly figure of a young girl wearing red shoes walking on the top floor of the building. On 15 April 2004 the paper covered a story about a couple who called in a vicar to bless their house after months of ghostly occurrences. The lights and television would switch on and off, and sensations of coldness and the aroma of perfume could be detected.
- A very old legend dating back to the twelfth century is regarding the Black Horse of Scarborough. This is not a pub but the ghost of a horse that has haunted the town for over 800 years. It was originally seen galloping near to the town and reports over the centuries have told of how the sky turns black and is then followed by a thunderstorm shortly after the horse has been sighted.

Scarborough Castle

Scarborough Castle was built in the reign of King Stephen (r. 1135-1154). Prior to this the site was used as a Roman signal station. The ruins of the castle sit on a high promontory more than 300ft above the level of the sea at the eastern end of the town. It is a dramatic site with a rich history that has endured sieges and damage during the Civil War by Parliamentary forces. In December 1914 the town and castle came under German naval bombardment which killed seventeen people and injured eighty others. The barracks at the castle, built in 1745, was completely destroyed.

One of the most famous episodes in the castle's history concerned King Edward II's (r. 1307-1327) favourite and lover, Piers Gaveston, the Earl of Cornwall. The instability of Edward's reign was reflected in the constant feud with the barons of England who complained about many issues concerning Edward's rule, especially the influence of Gaveston. A commission appointed by the king in 1311 proposed checks to balance the power of the Crown, which included the exile of Gaveston. Edward had little choice but to obey the ordinance and exile his favourite. However, it was not for very long and Gaveston was recalled in 1312. The hatred towards him from the barons cannot be overestimated. The barons included Thomas, Earl of Lancaster, the king's first cousin; the Earl of Pembroke; the Earl of Warren; and the former governor of Scarborough Castle, Henry de Percy. They were furious that Gaveston was back in the country and they decided to take matters into their hands. They marched to York in pursuit of him but Gaveston fled to Newcastle and there went by ship to Scarborough where Edward had made him governor of Scarborough Castle. The Earls of Pembroke and Warren, along with Henry de Percy, took their army to Scarborough where they soon captured Gaveston. This marked the end of Piers Gaveston. He was dragged, kicking and screaming, before having his head removed with an axe at Blacklow Hill, 1 mile outside of Warwick. The king was outraged and took revenge on Scarborough by placing the town under the repressive authority of appointed governors.

Gaveston's headless and malevolent ghost famously haunts the ruins of Scarborough Castle, where he tries to lure people over the edge of the castle down the cliffs in the hope that one of them will fall to their death. Visitors to the castle have recalled feelings of being pushed and hearing the voice of a man laughing.

The Lancaster Inn, Scarborough.

St Mary's Church, Scarborough.

Scarborough Castle.

Scarborough Castle and the cliffs.

Another ghost who is said to haunt the castle is that of an old woman in grey, thought to be the wife of the castle gun keeper. She was regularly seen around her former home and staff reported feeling uneasy in the Master Gunner's House. The woman's appearance was disturbing to visitors, so much so that an exorcism was performed.

Staithes

Staithes was home to Captain James Cook, where he worked as a grocer's apprentice. It is a small fishing town with its own bay, and the surrounding cliffs tend to encroach on the town. It is about 9 miles north of Whitby.

In his *The History and Antiquities of Cleveland* (1846), John Walker Ord told of the following ghost story that took place at Staithes. A poor fisherman by the name of Harrison accidentally fell 600ft over a cliff to his death. Shortly afterwards, locals told how they were frightened by visitations of the ghost that appeared during the day as well as night. Harrison's relatives visited the unhappy ghost and spoke to it. They confirmed that it was Harrison in every detail – dress and appearance. Eventually, a Roman Catholic priest was asked to perform an exorcism to banish the ghost. The ritual worked, as Harrison's ghost was never seen again.

Staithes is also known for the ghost of young Hannah Grundy, who has been seen walking along the cliff side. Hannah died when the cliffs crumbled beneath her in the early nineteenth century.

When people speak of Whitby, they naturally comment on the usual landmarks and features but also the atmosphere of the place. It certainly does have an atmosphere – a good one. It's what makes it the unique place that it is. In addition, it has the added bonus of being complemented by fine surroundings. For such a small town, it has a fascinating history as well as many tales and legends of the supernatural. No doubt there are many other stories and experiences still to be told.

Other titles published by The History Press

Whitby: Then & Now (The Second Selection)
COLIN WATERS

The historic town of Whitby has long inspired photographers and artists to try to capture the essence of the town. In this second selection of more than eighty nostalgic images, Colin Waters once again captures life in the area as it once was – and as it is now, revealing the changes Whitby has witnessed and providing a fascinating insight into a way of life now lost.

978 0 7524 4657 8

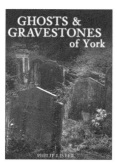

Ghosts & Gravestones of York
PHILIP LISTER

Join Yorkshire guide Philip Lister as he takes you on a tour of York's dark and ghostly side. Discover the fascinating history of the Minster and the legend of the haunted pew, the story of the terrible massacre at Bedern Orphanage, and the stories behind the sightless severed heads which have throughout history gazed down on the citizens of York from Micklegate Bar.

978 0 7524 4357 7

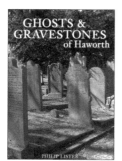

Ghosts & Gravestones of Haworth
PHILIP LISTER

Join local guide Philip Lister as he takes you on a tour of Haworth's dark and ghostly side: meet the ghost of Room 7 at the Old White Lion Hotel, the Grey Lady of Weavers Restaurant, the Ponden Hall's harbinger of doom, Old Greybeard. – and don't miss the Graveyard Cookbook, a veritable feast of ghoulish delights!

978 0 7524 3958 7

Haunted Middlesbrough
TINA LAKIN

This creepy collection of true-life tales takes the reader on a tour through the streets of Middlesbrough. Drawing on historical and contemporary sources, it unearths a chilling range of supernatural phenomena, from poltergeists in Stockton Town Hall and ghostly gardeners at Albert Park to Victorian spirits in Linthorpe Road. Illustrated with more than fifty archive photographs, this book will delight anyone with an interest in the paranormal history of the area.

978 0 7524 4193 1

Visit our website and discover thousands of other History Press books. **www.thehistorypress.co.uk**